WITHDRAWN

CUBA *and the* COMING AMERICAN REVOLUTION

WITHDRAWN

CUBA and the COMING AMERICAN REVOLUTION

JACK BARNES

PATHFINDER

New York   London   Montreal   Sydney

Edited by Steve Clark

Copyright © 2001 by Pathfinder Press
ISBN 0-87348-930-6 paper; ISBN 0-87348-932-2 cloth
Library of Congress Control Number: 2001090514

Manufactured in the United States of America

First edition, 2001

COVER DESIGN: Eva Braiman
COVER: Hans Hofmann, *Fantasia,* 1943, oil, duco and casein on plywood,
51.5 x 36.625 inches, University of California, Berkeley Art Museum;
gift of the artist. Photographed for the UC Berkeley Art Museum by
Benjamin Blackwell.

Pathfinder
410 West Street, New York, NY 10014, U.S.A.
Fax: (212) 727-0150
E-mail: pathfinderpress@compuserve.com

PATHFINDER DISTRIBUTORS AROUND THE WORLD:
Australia (and Asia and the Pacific):
Pathfinder, 176 Redfern St., 1st floor, Redfern, NSW 2016
Postal address: P.O. Box K879, Haymarket, NSW 1240

Canada:
Pathfinder, 2761 Dundas St. West, Toronto, ON, M6P 1Y4

Iceland:
Pathfinder, Klapparstíg 26, 2d floor, 101 Reykjavík
Postal address: P. Box 0233, IS 121 Reykjavík

New Zealand:
Pathfinder, P.O. Box 3025, Auckland

Sweden:
Pathfinder, Domargränd 16, S-129 47 Hägersten

United Kingdom (and Europe, Africa except South Africa, and Middle East):
Pathfinder, 47 The Cut, London, SE1 8LL

United States (and Caribbean, Latin America, and South Africa):
Pathfinder, 410 West Street, New York, NY 10014

Contents

About the author

JACK BARNES has been national secretary of the Socialist Workers Party since 1972. Beginning in the mid-1970s he carried central responsibility for the political turn of the SWP toward opportunities to get the overwhelming majority of its members and leaders into the industrial trade unions. From that base, party members have built the communist movement while actively engaged with fellow workers in efforts to transform the unions into revolutionary instruments of struggle that defend not only their own membership but the interests of workers and farmers worldwide. The 1978–91 record of this turn in building proletarian parties in the United States and other countries is published in *The Changing Face of U.S. Politics*.

Since 1998 Barnes has led a second major campaign of the SWP and its sister organizations internationally to turn toward the openings brought by the toughening resistance and increasing geographical spread of vanguard actions by workers and farmers standing up to the bosses' drive to increase profits on the backs of the producers. The opening of this second turn is recorded in "A Sea Change in Working-Class Politics," the first chapter of *Capitalism's World Disorder*.

An organizer of the Fair Play for Cuba Committee and actions in defense of Black rights, Barnes joined the Young Socialist Alliance in 1960 and the Socialist Workers Party in 1961. He organized the successful four-year-long effort to defend three members of the YSA in Bloomington, Indiana, indicted in May 1963 for advocating the overthrow of the state of Indiana by force and violence. In 1965 he was elected national chairperson of the Young Socialist Alliance and became the director of the SWP and YSA's work in the growing movement against the Vietnam War. He has been a member of the National Committee of the Socialist Workers Party since 1963 and a national officer of the party since 1969. From 1963 on he has carried major responsibilities for the party's international work.

Parallel to his responsibilities as an organizer, Barnes has been a contributing editor to *New International*, a magazine of Marxist politics and theory. He is the author of many books, pamphlets, and articles, a number of which are listed at the front of the book.

■

MARY-ALICE WATERS, who authored the preface, is editor of *New International* and president of Pathfinder Press. She has been a member of the Socialist Workers Party since 1964 and of the SWP National Committee since 1967, and has carried central responsibilities for the party's international work. Joining the Young Socialist Alliance in 1962, she was editor of the *Young Socialist* (1966–67) and served as YSA national secretary and then national chairperson (1967–68).

In the early 1970s Waters was editor of the *Militant* newsweekly. Waters is the author of *Pathfinder Was Born with the October Revolution, Che Guevara and the Imperialist Reality, Feminism and the Marxist Movement*, "Background to the Coup in Algeria," and many other pamphlets and articles. She edited and contributed to numerous Pathfinder titles, including: *Playa Girón/Bay of Pigs: Washington's First Military Defeat in the Americas; Che Guevara Talks to Young People; Rosa Luxemburg Speaks; The Changing Face of U.S. Politics; Capitalism's World Disorder; Cosmetics, Fashions, and the Exploitation of Women; Communist Continuity and the Fight for Women's Liberation;* and *To Speak the Truth: Why Washington's 'Cold War' Against Cuba Doesn't End.*

Preface

"The victory at Playa Girón punctured the myth of U.S. imperialism's invincibility. It left us with the conviction that the Cuban Revolution would be at the center of the class struggle inside the United States as long as the working class was in power in Cuba, and we had become convinced that such would be the case for the rest of our lives."

Jack Barnes
March 2001

IN LESS THAN SEVENTY-TWO HOURS OF COMBAT in April 1961 near the Bay of Pigs, Cuba's Revolutionary Air Force, militias, police, and Rebel Army defeated an invasion by 1,500 Cuban counterrevolutionaries armed, trained, scripted, and deployed by Washington. The stunning victory, Yankee imperialism's first military defeat in the Americas, had repercussions around the world—not least of all within the United States itself.

Jack Barnes takes that historic moment as his starting point for *Cuba and the Coming American Revolution*. It was the moment when Cuba no longer appeared as yet another victim of the most powerful country in history, but emerged as its equal. This is, at the same time, a book about the struggles of working people in the imperialist heartland, the youth who are attracted to them, and the example set by the people of Cuba, who taught us that revolution is not only necessary—it can be made. It is a book about the unshakable confidence the workers and farmers of Cuba gave us in what working people are capable of. "The greatest obstacle to the line of march of the toilers," notes the author in the pages that follow, "is the tendency, promoted and perpetuated by the exploiting classes, for working people to underestimate ourselves, to underestimate what we can accomplish, to doubt our own worth." What the workers and farmers of Cuba showed us is that with class solidarity, political consciousness, courage, focused and persistent efforts at education, and a revolutionary leadership of high caliber like that in Cuba, tested and forged in battle over the years, it is possible to stand up to enormous might and seemingly insurmountable odds *and win*.

That was the lesson internalized in the early 1960s by a vanguard of young people inside the United States aided, encouraged, and educated by veteran workers and farmers of the Socialist Workers Party. Their story is told here in "1961: Year of Education." Written as the foreword to the recently released Pathfinder book, *Playa Girón/Bay of Pigs: Washington's First Military Defeat in the Americas*, it describes the impact of the Cuban Revolution on youth who were already being radicalized by the deepening mass struggle to bring down the "Jim Crow" system of segregation in the U.S. South and roll back other forms of racist discrimination throughout the country. It recounts the work of the students who established a campus chapter of the Fair Play for Cuba Committee at Carleton College in Minnesota in the decisive few months culminating in the April 19 victory at Playa Girón, a committee that in the heat of events briefly became the largest campus chapter in the country. It describes the class-struggle lessons young people learned as they went through these experiences and tells how they began building the Young Socialist Alliance in the course of this work.

The second piece published here, "There Will Be a Victorious Revolution in the United States before a Victorious Counterrevolution in Cuba," is based on talks given by Barnes in both New York City and Seattle in March 2001 at meetings to celebrate the publication of *Playa Girón/Bay of Pigs*. Among the 450 participants in these gatherings were dozens of volunteers from one end of the country to the other whose labor made possible the rapid, quality production of the book. The audiences spanned the generations from those who were already active partisans of the Cuban Revolution at the time of the Bay of Pigs to socialist youth who are today making this chapter of history their own.

Playa Girón/Bay of Pigs came off the presses in both Spanish and English just in time to be launched at a March 22–24 conference in Havana on "Girón: 40 Years Later" and given by the Cuban hosts to each participant. During that event the political and military leaders of revolutionary Cuba whose guidance had assured the victory, including commander in chief Fidel Castro, joined to discuss the events that occurred four decades earlier with a U.S. delegation some of whose members either fought as part of the U.S.-trained and -financed Brigade 2506, helped prepare the CIA invasion plans, or acted as apologists and advisers for the administration of President John F. Kennedy.

Other activities marking the Cuban victory at the Bay of Pigs took place in numerous U.S. cities, from Miami to New York, from Seattle to Minneapolis to Boston. At each of them the focus was not only to tell the story of what happened many years ago, but to use that knowledge to understand the world today and prepare for coming battles.

Why do the U.S. rulers remain as ferociously determined to try to crush the Cuban Revolution as they were in 1961? It isn't complicated. The first free territory of the Americas still stands as a revolutionary and a socialist example for the oppressed and exploited the world over.

U.S. secretary of state Colin Powell explained it more accurately than he perhaps intended before an April 26 House Appropriations subcommittee hearing in Washington, responding to a question about why the United States government refuses to alter its unbending hostility toward Cuba. In China, Russia, and Vietnam, Powell replied, "you can see leaders who the world is changing." But in Cuba, he said, Castro "hasn't changed his views in any way."

Mr. Secretary got it right, just as each of his predecessors has. The people of Cuba have never surrendered. Their message to would-be invaders remains the same: If you come, you stay. They will not subordinate the interests of working people to the prerogatives of capital. They stand ready, as always, to aid revolutionary struggles wherever they may occur, by any means necessary.

■

The most important response to the publication of *Playa Girón/Bay of Pigs* came from new generations of readers who discovered something unanticipated in its pages. They had expected a clear and readable account of the historic battle from José Ramón Fernández, who led the main column of troops that defeated the invasion forces in April 1961. They had expected the truth and class clarity of the political leadership given the people of Cuba and the world in the speeches by Fidel Castro, Ernesto Che Guevara, and Raúl Castro. They had expected to find expressed in the pages of the book the determination and courage of the workers and peasants, overwhelmingly young, who fought and died on the road to Playa Girón to defend the first socialist revolution in our hemisphere.

The surprise was learning how a previous generation of young socialists inside the United States had waged an intense political battle in defense of the Cuban Revolution right here in the weeks leading up to, during, and after the U.S.-organized invasion. This previously unrecorded chapter in the history of the communist youth movement was to its continuators today not just an interesting account of something long past, however, but a model of mass work to be emulated now.

After reading "1961: Year of Education," several young socialists in Pittsburgh even decided to rent the video and organize a gathering to watch *Salt of the Earth*—the famous blacklisted movie about the unionization battle of largely Mexican zinc miners in the U.S. Southwest in the 1950s. Showing the movie and discussing it with one of the union organizers was among the activities organized in the months preceding the Bay of Pigs invasion by Carleton College students who were meeting weekly in a socialist discussion club, building a campus Fair Play for Cuba chapter, and rapidly becoming young communists. It was part of the broad education campaign that helped to politicize a layer of young people and prepare the ground for the response to U.S. aggression against Cuba. If the movie in 1961 stimulated the kind of political controversy and education indicated, the Pittsburgh young socialists surmised, then it must still be worth seeing. The movie, they thought, might be timely, and ring especially true, given the growing vanguard contributions of immigrant workers throughout the U.S. labor movement and the militancy today of union coal miners in that same part of the country, many of whom are Navajo, Mexican, or Chicano.

Most important, these young socialists *acted* on their conclusions.

■

I was one of the students at Carleton College for whom the defeat of U.S. imperialism at the Bay of Pigs was a watershed, and whose life course was changed by the activities of the people described in the opening chapter of this book. Before that sophomore year in college I had virtually no interest in politics. Had eighteen-year-olds been allowed to vote in the 1960 U.S. presidential elections, I would probably have cast a ballot for Richard Nixon. (Lowering the voting age to eighteen was an extension of the franchise only conceded a decade after that by the U.S. rulers, as they vainly sought to defuse the growing mass outrage among young people against being used as cannon fodder in the Vietnam War.)

Six months later I called myself a socialist, even though as yet I only vaguely understood what that might be.

In the months leading up to the Bay of Pigs invasion, I attended few of the programs organized by the student government–sponsored Challenge program described by Jack Barnes in "1961: Year of Education." I missed the meeting at which national Fair Play for Cuba Committee organizers Robert Williams and Ed Shaw spoke, for example, because I had a paper to write or an exam to prepare for. I enjoyed the study of English literature and took it seriously! But the next day the entire campus was discussing that electrifying meeting. Like others who had not been there, it had an impact on me nonetheless.

As did hundreds of students at Carleton, I avidly followed the political propaganda war being fought out on the bulletin board in the Student Union, reading the daily newspaper and magazine clippings posted by the Fair Play for Cuba Committee as well as those put up by critics or enemies of the revolution.

A Fair Play supporter gave me a copy of C. Wright Mills's *Listen, Yankee*, which I devoured in one sitting. That slim paperback written by a radical professor—a socialist-minded, motorcycle-riding, heart-attack-prone, pure product of America who staunchly opposed Washington's policy toward Cuba—was not only my introduction to the history of Cuba's anticolonial and anti-imperialist struggle. It also opened my eyes to the arrogance and brutality of U.S. imperialist domination of Latin America. I began to think about and discuss with others what we in the United States who opposed that reality needed to do.

Like millions in Cuba before me, in the spring of 1961 I became a "Fidelista" before I was yet knowingly a "socialista." I was a bit like the teenage antiaircraft artillery gunners in Cuba quoted in an article in the April 23 issue of the *Militant* newspaper. They described their reactions after listening to the speech by Fidel Castro hours before the battle of Playa Girón began, when he talked for the first time about the socialist character of the revolution in Cuba. "We didn't understand well what socialism was," one said, but "someone declared that if Fidel was a socialist, then we were socialists too, and everyone there agreed with that."

The night of April 19, 1961, as word spread across campus of Washington's crushing defeat at what we knew back then as Cochinos Bay, I joined in the celebration of our victory and never turned back.

The deepening revolution in Cuba was not isolated in the world of the early 1960s. Other powerful anti-imperialist struggles were advancing too, from Indochina to the Congo to Panama. Mass battles to bring down Jim Crow segregation in the United States were a form of these international struggles and, at the same time, drew strength from them. There were new stirrings among Mexican-Americans and Chicanos as well. In my own case it was the Algerian Revolution that had the deepest impact.

A few months after the Bay of Pigs, I found myself in France for the new academic year. The Algerian independence struggle, paid for in blood by some one million Algerians, was rapidly approaching victory. The great movie depiction of this struggle, *Battle of Algiers*, captures much of the courage and determination of the Algerian people, as well as the immeasurable brutality of the French imperialist forces. No one should miss it.

Paris resembled a city under siege during the closing months of the war. In the wake of a failed coup attempt, the Secret Army Organization (OAS), a clandestine fascist group based in the officer corps of the French army, had unleashed a campaign of bombings and assassinations in the capital aimed at bringing down the French government before it recognized Algerian independence. Paratroops armed with submachine guns stood guard twenty-four hours a day on every street corner, and plastic bombs exploded nightly in mailboxes and other public locations throughout the city.

Student antifascist committees were active in every faculty. They regularly organized demonstrations challenging the prohibition on street actions. Facing off against the much-hated special police force, the CRS, they inevitably sustained injuries and arrests. In February 1962 eight demonstrators were trampled and suffocated to death as those escaping a CRS attack fled into an abandoned metro station from which there was no exit. More than a million people poured into Paris streets to join the funeral cortege to the Père Lachaise cemetery, where the martyrs of the Paris Commune are also buried. Despite the casualties still to come, the war was over. The people of Algeria had won. A few months later the Evian Accords were signed, ceding independence to Algeria after more than 130 years of French colonial rule. A workers and farmers government soon came to power, with National Liberation Front leader Ahmed Ben Bella at its head.

Joining these student demonstrations was my first direct experience with the terror of police brutality and the reality of fascist violence. It was a political education that left an indelible impression. Unbeknown to me at the time, the student antifascist committees, whose actions in the streets of Paris were indispensable to mobilizing support for Algerian independence, were led by my own comrades, young people in the leadership of the left wing of the Union des Etudiants Communistes (UEC—Communist Students Union). These youth were soon to be expelled from the UEC at the insistence of the leadership of the French Communist Party, in part for leading these actions, and they founded the Jeunesse Communiste Révolutionnaire (JCR—Revolutionary Communist Youth), the sister organization of the Young Socialist Alliance.

When I returned to Carleton for my senior year, I immediately joined the Young Socialist Alliance without the slightest doubt that a disciplined communist organization was necessary to meet similar conditions that were sure to be produced by capitalism in the United States.

The liberation struggle in Algeria had an impact on layers of young people and fighters against oppression far beyond North Africa and France, of course, including in the United States. Malcolm X was one of them. At a May 1964 meeting of the Militant Labor Forum in New York City, Malcolm pointed out that while only a few years earlier Ben Bella had been in the prisons of French imperialism, "today they have to negotiate with him because he knew that the one thing he had on his side was truth and time. Time is on the side of the oppressed today, it's against the oppressor. Truth is on the side of the oppressed today, it's against the oppressor." During both of his trips to Africa and the Middle East in 1964, Malcolm traveled to Algeria to meet with fellow revolutionaries.

There were strong ties connecting the Algerian and Cuban revolutions. The years immediately following independence from France saw close and growing collaboration between Havana and Algiers to aid anti-imperialist struggles from the Congo to Argentina to apartheid South Africa, and to defend the Algerian and Cuban revolutions.

In the fall of 1962 Ben Bella came to New York City to address the United Nations General Assembly on the occasion of Algeria being admitted to that body as an independent nation. From there Ben Bella traveled to Washington for a brief state visit with President John F. Kennedy, and then, despite the open threats of his hosts, demonstratively flew straight on to Havana, where he joined his comrades-in-arms. In an account written thirty-five years later, Ben Bella recalled that he arrived in Havana on October 16, the very eve of the Cuban "Missile" Crisis, "amid indescribable scenes of popular enthusiasm" for the revolution and its solidarity with Algeria.

The first large-scale internationalist mission of Cuban volunteers was the dispatch of tanks and a column of troops under the command of Efigenio Ameijeiras, the head of the Revolutionary National Police battalion that had fought so tenaciously at Playa Girón; they went to Algeria in October 1963 to help the revolutionary government repel a U.S.-backed invasion by Moroccan troops.

With the overthrow of the Ben Bella–led workers and farmers government in June 1965, the defeat of the anti-imperialist forces in the Congo later that same year, and the withdrawal from the Congo of the Cuban volunteer troops headed by Che

Guevara, the era of that type of close collaboration between Havana and Algiers came to an end.

■

More than forty years have passed since the last victorious socialist revolution. That is a long time, not on the historical scale, but in political time. A great deal has changed in the world. We don't have to look far or delve that deeply, however, to see within the United States social forces being propelled into motion that are capable of transforming themselves as they come to realize in struggle that we need the same kind of revolution that the workers and peasants of Cuba carried to victory. From the streets of Cincinnati to the coal mines on the Navajo Nation, from the farm cooperatives of southern Georgia to the dairy farms of Wisconsin, from the port of Charleston to the packinghouses of Omaha, from the fields of California's Imperial Valley to the garment shops of Los Angeles and New York, as the pages that follow explain, "a vanguard layer of workers and farmers in this country is becoming more confident from their common fighting experience and thus more open to considering radical ideas, including the program and strategy of the modern communist movement. Whether they know it yet or not, their own experience in life and struggle is bringing them closer to that of the workers and peasants of revolutionary Cuba."

This is not an ideological question but a practical one, a question of proletarian integrity, habits of discipline, and morality—of Marxism.

We've been reminded of that in recent weeks by the profound class divide that has opened once again in the United States following the acknowledgment by former Democratic U.S. senator Robert Kerrey of the civilian massacre he was responsible for more than thirty years ago in Vietnam. (He was moved to "bare his soul" just days before the story was to be printed in the *New York Times* and broadcast nationwide on CBS's *Sixty*

Minutes!) Liberals are wailing about the personal agony Kerrey has been obliged to live with 'lo these many decades—"the bad war made him do it." Meanwhile conservatives intone phrases about the "realities" of battle, defending the "free-fire zones" where every Vietnamese man, woman, and child was assumed to be "the enemy." Kerrey's only betrayal, as far as they are concerned, was later becoming a Democratic Party officeholder.

The bipartisan sanctimonious posturing should serve to remind us not only of the enormous price paid in blood by the people of Vietnam to gain their independence, but also of the example of the Rebel Army during the battle at Playa Girón, where not one prisoner, by the invaders' own testimony, was mistreated or abused, denied food, water, or medical treatment equivalent to that available to the Cuban troops. The same was true throughout the entire two years of the revolutionary war in Cuba where, despite the record of the Batista regime's brutal killers and torturers, no captured government soldier was treated by the Rebel Army with anything but humanity and respect.

What determined the outcome at Playa Girón, as in Vietnam and Algeria, was ultimately not which side had the superior armaments, but the class character of the contending forces and what they were fighting for. That's what the U.S. rulers did not and can never understand. They did their mathematical calculations, as Che Guevara is quoted saying here, but they failed to measure the moral relationship of forces. "They have always been wrong about us," Guevara concluded. "They always arrive late."

They still are wrong about the capacities of the toilers, and they still always arrive late. And always will.

That class line is what hundreds of workers and farmers, and young people on dozens of campuses in the United States, were responding to during the recent speaking engagements by two Cuban youth leaders, Javier Dueñas and Yanelis Martínez. Their month-long visit to the United States took place as this book was being prepared. In talking about the opportunities and challenges facing working people and youth in Cuba today, in responding to what they saw and learned of the U.S. class struggle, and in answering the questions put to them everywhere about the world and the future ahead of us all, these young Cubans kept shifting the focus to the ordinary workers, farmers, and young people just awakening to political life in both Cuba and the United States. Above all, the two Cubans pointed to the capacities of working people and youth attracted to their struggles to rise to the level of consciousness, discipline, courage, and class solidarity necessary to take their own future in hand. This is what the people of Cuba have done, the example they've set, for the last forty-odd years.

"What is special is never the human material," says the author in the pages that follow, "but the times we live in and our degree of preparation. If we've worked together beforehand to build a disciplined, centralized workers party—with a program and strategy that advances the historic line of march of our class worldwide—then we'll be ready for new opportunities in the class struggle when they explode in totally unanticipated ways. We'll be prepared to build a mass proletarian combat party that can take on the capitalist rulers in revolutionary struggle and defeat them. That is the most important lesson that every one of us can draw."

If the victory of the people of Cuba at Playa Girón is still stuck in Washington's craw some forty years later, it is not because of something that happened long ago or miles away. It is because of the present and the future right here in the United States, where, as Jack Barnes concludes in the opening chapter of this book, the revolutionary capacities of the workers and farmers are "as utterly discounted by the ruling powers as were those of the peasant and proletarian masses of Cuba. And just as wrongly."

That is what *Cuba and the Coming American Revolution* is about.

Mary-Alice Waters
May 2001

1961: Year of Education

"The October Crisis was a continuation of the U.S. fiasco at Girón. The defeat they suffered there led them to risk an atomic war. Girón was like a bone sticking in their throats, something they don't accept to this day. In war one either wins or loses. But they can't admit having lost in their efforts to dominate such a small country."

Division General Enrique Carreras
Revolutionary Armed Forces of Cuba
October 1997

ON THE MORNING OF APRIL 18, 1961, readers of daily newspapers across the United States woke up to front-page headlines proclaiming, "Rebels Near Havana, Invade Four Provinces." An Associated Press news dispatch reported that "Cuban rebel forces" had landed within thirty-eight miles of Havana and at numerous other points on the island. Citing a press release from the "Cuban Revolutionary Council," the dispatch said that much of the Cuban militia had already defected to the invading forces and "in the next few hours" the deciding battle for the country would be fought. "Rebel" forces were "in control

First published in March 2001 in the *Militant* newsweekly, the above is the foreword to *Playa Girón/Bay of Pigs: Washington's First Military Defeat in the Americas* by Fidel Castro and José Ramón Fernández.

of the Isle of Pines and had freed some 10,000 political prisoners held there."

Most Americans took the story as good coin, expecting to soon hear that the "pro-Communist dictator" Fidel Castro had been ousted.

Around the country, however, in dozens of cities and on a number of college campuses, there were pockets of individuals who knew from the beginning that every word of the AP story was a lie. We had been carrying out an intensive educational campaign for weeks. We were getting ready for the invasion we knew was coming, preparing to act here in the Yankee heartland side by side with the Cuban people the moment it was launched. Between April 17 and April 19, as the battle was being fought in Cuba, we confidently took to the streets, organized speak-outs, posted marked-up newspaper clippings, and went on the radio asserting that, all press reports to the contrary, the U.S. government-organized and -financed invasion was being defeated, not winning.

As we had been doing for months, we pointed to the immense popularity of the revolution among the Cuban people in response to the measures the new government was organizing them to take. The Mafia-run gambling dens and brothels, a national shame, had been shut down. Land had been distributed to more than 100,000 tenant farmers, sharecroppers, and squatters. House and apartment rents, as well as electricity and telephone rates, had been slashed. Racial discrimination was outlawed and equal access not only made law but also enforced. Public beaches, previously off limits to Blacks, had been opened to all. A nationwide campaign to eliminate illiteracy had been launched—part of a broader extension of public education to the countryside, among the poor, and for women. Popular militias had formed in factories, other workplaces, schools, neighborhoods, and towns across the island, as Cubans demanded arms and military training to defend their new conquests. The huge money-gouging U.S. monopolies had been nationalized, as well as the major landed, commercial, and industrial property holdings of the wealthy Cuban families who had been the social and political base of the Batista dictatorship.

Through more than two years of popular mobilization, the workers and farmers of Cuba had begun transforming not only their country but themselves, we explained. It was precisely for this reason that Cubans could, and would, fight to the death to defend their revolution—and do so successfully.

Only thirty-six hours after the initial AP stories made headlines across the United States, the counterrevolutionary "rebel forces"—who had landed not thirty-eight miles from Havana or on the Isle of Pines, but near the Bay of Pigs on the southern coast of the island—had been ignominiously routed at Playa Girón by Cuba's popular militias, Revolutionary National Police, Revolutionary Air Force, and Rebel Army. Not only the decisiveness, but also the speed of the April defeat was stunning. The strategic plan authorized by President John F. Kennedy called for the 1,500-man mercenary force at least to establish and hold a beachhead on an isolated slice of Cuban territory long enough to declare a provisional government and appeal for direct military intervention by Washington and its closest allies in Latin America.

The shock of this very first military defeat of U.S. imperialism in the Americas began to register in Washington, and among its defenders in pressrooms, factories, and schools across the country. In the weeks that followed, as bitter and self-serving recriminations among organizers of the invasion spilled out, more and more information about the U.S.-run military operation and the social background of the individual Cuban "freedom fighters" began to make its way into the mainstream press in the United States.

As these facts became known, supporters of the Cuban Revolution took full advantage to spread the truth, point to the accuracy of what we had been arguing for months, and underline the sober exactitude of the speeches and statements of leaders of the Cuban Revolution over the previous two years.

The first issue of *Time* magazine to appear after the Cuban victory, for example, revealed that the purported authors of the Cuban Revolutionary Council press release cited so authoritatively by AP, including "prestigious" figures such as José Miró Cardona, not only knew nothing of the timing of the invasion but had actually been held as quasi-prisoners by the U.S. government while the operation was under way. The press release issued in their name had in fact been written by the CIA officers in charge of the invasion, while the members of the CIA-created Cuban government-in-exile were held incommunicado under military guard in a barracks at the deserted Opa-Locka airfield near Miami.

Both the AP wire story and *Time* magazine article, and the use we made of them, were part of the intense debate that raged on a number of campuses, as well as in factories, rail yards, and other workplaces throughout the United States during the opening years of the Cuban Revolution. It was a propaganda battle that, from one end of the country to the other, became a confrontation in the streets both during the days surrounding the U.S.-organized invasion at the Bay of Pigs and a year and a half later during the October "Missile" Crisis.

This political battle that began more than forty years ago was one that changed the lives of a not-insignificant number of young people in the United States. It transformed the communist movement here in a way that paralleled the profound changes taking place in Cuba and elsewhere around the world. Nothing since the October 1917 Bolshevik Revolution in Russia has had such an impact.

There are moments in history when everything ceases to be "normal." Suddenly the speed of events and stakes involved intensify every word and action. Neutral ground seems to disappear. Alignments shift and new forces come together. The polite conventions of civil discourse that normally reign in bourgeois circles evaporate, including within the "academic community."

April 1961, when the bombing and invasion of Cuba by mercenaries organized, financed, and deployed by Washington met the fearless resistance and lightning victory of the Cuban people, was such a moment.

■

At the time I was one of the organizers of the campus Fair Play for Cuba Committee (FPCC) at Carleton College, a small, very respectable liberal arts school in Northfield, Minnesota, well south of the twin cities of Minneapolis-St. Paul. The billboard at the Northfield city limits welcomed visitors to "Cows, Colleges, and Contentment." The contentment was sorely tried by the rise of the Cuban Revolution and by the historic and irreconcilable conflict of class forces reflected at the Bay of Pigs. The cows continued to fare well.

The experiences we went through at Carleton were not unique. To one degree or another they were repeated at several dozen colleges and universities across the United States.

The January 1959 victory of the Cuban Revolution, combined with Washington's intense hostility to the economic and social transformation being wrought so close to U.S. shores, led three Carleton students to decide to visit Cuba in 1960, each at different times, to see for themselves. I was one of them, spending the summer in Cuba to study the economic changes taking place there. I was deeply affected by these ten weeks of daily participation together with other young people and with the workers and farmers of Cuba in actions that constituted one of the most important turning points of the revolution. Returning for my senior year, I was determined to find those in the United States whose response to what was happening in Cuba was similar to mine. I had two intertwined goals: to work together with whomever possible to oppose Washington's attempts to crush the Cuban Revolution, and to find among them those who wanted to organize their lives to emulate here the example set by the Rebel Army and Cuba's working people.

From the spring of 1960 on, every political person in the world knew an invasion of Cuba was imminent. Reports about the CIA recruitment and training facilities in Florida, Louisiana, and Guatemala circulated for months. Despite heavy government pressure on mostly pliant journalists and publishers alike, bits and pieces of news found their way into print. Cuba's foreign minister, Raúl Roa, speaking before United Nations bodies at least three times, publicly detailed the scope of the preparations under way. He made it clear beyond challenge that the only question was exactly when and where the invasion would occur, not whether.

Under the impact of experiences in Cuba, some students at Carleton organized a socialist study group on campus to read and discuss Marxist theory—from *The German Ideology* and other early works by Karl Marx that had recently been published in English translation for the first time, to the *Communist Manifesto*, to works by communist leaders in the United States. We organized other students to subscribe to the *Militant* newsweekly—which we had begun reading in Cuba and was our most thorough, regular, and reliable source of information about the revolution.

Early in 1961, convinced the invasion could not be more than weeks away, we organized a campus chapter of the Fair Play for Cuba Committee, and began to carry out virtually nonstop political education activities to lay the groundwork for deepening and broadening opposition to Washington's plans.

The bulletin board in the student union soon became a battleground. Every day we posted clippings with the latest news reports appearing in the big-business dailies and weeklies, from the *Minneapolis Tribune* to *Newsweek*. They were marked up and annotated to underscore Washington's acts of aggression against Cuba and to expose the fabrications and self-contradictory information emanating from U.S. government sources. We also tacked up speeches by Cuban leaders that we clipped out of the *Militant*, and we made the unqualified assertion that their assessment of the U.S. rulers' response to the advance of the revolution would soon be proven correct. Opponents of the revolution, from liberals to ultra-right-wingers, would reply by posting articles they thought bolstered their views; we would answer the next day, often using the very same sources to expose their arguments. We were learning a valuable lesson about the existence, and effectiveness, of imperialist disinformation campaigns.

No one tried to tear down clippings or halt the debate, however, which we counted as our first victory. We had done what communists in plants and mills across the country were simultaneously doing: we had taken the moral high ground, proving that defenders of Cuba, not our opponents, were the ones pressing for debate, for openness, for reading the press critically and discussing the facts.

In February 1961 we had initiated a series of public meetings on Cuba. These programs were sponsored by Challenge, a lecture series we had established earlier in the school year after winning support from the student government for the initiative. The campus newspaper, the *Carletonian*, described the program as designed to "challenge the underlying beliefs and assumptions of the student body by bringing to the campus 'numerous intelligent and committed individuals who hold dissenting views which are not heard by the Carleton student body.'"

Challenge had already had a broad impact on campus. It organized debates on U.S. covert operations in Laos. Marxist literary critic Annette Rubinstein, an editor of *Science and Society* magazine, had lectured on Shakespeare. Challenge sponsored a debate on the May 1960 San Francisco "riots" against the so-called House Un-American Activities Committee (HUAC). We held a showing and discussion of *Salt of the Earth*, the blacklisted movie about the unionization battle of largely Mexican zinc miners in the Southwest in face of posse violence and ferocious red-baiting. A member of the International Union of Mine, Mill, and Smelters Workers spoke after the film about their 1950 strike and ongoing battle against the mine operators. Another program on the unions—an "unknown institution" at Carleton in those years—featured Mark Starr, the longtime education director of the International Ladies' Garment Workers' Union.

All these events were controversial on campus. But nothing compared to what broke out around programs on Cuba.

A letter to the editor in the *Carletonian* in March 1961 complained of the "rude treatment" a visiting professor allegedly received from several students who had challenged him on the facts in response to statements he made about Cuba. He acknowledged at the Challenge meeting that he wasn't an authority on the subject and later had to admit to the student paper he had never even been to Cuba.

The following week two members of the National Fair Play for Cuba Committee spoke on campus about the Cuban Revolution and the deepening struggle for Black rights throughout the United States. One was Robert F. Williams, a founding member of Fair Play who two years earlier had been removed by top NAACP officials as president of the Monroe, North Carolina, chapter for organizing fellow Black war veterans into armed self-defense of their community against racist thugs and nightriders. The other speaker was Ed Shaw, Midwest organizer of Fair Play, who was a typesetter and member of the International Typographical Union from Detroit, as well as a leader of the Socialist Workers Party. That meeting had a powerful impact on campus. What impressed us above all was that Williams and Shaw each talked about both the struggle for Black rights and the Cuban Revolution with similar ease and insight.

The next week, four Carleton students who had visited or lived in Cuba—three of them organizers of the campus Fair Play for Cuba Committee—presented a slide show and debated the issues.

We organized to make sure that every issue of the *Carletonian* carried articles, letters, cartoons, and other commentary that was part of the deepening discussion about the Cuban Revolution among students and faculty. Jim Gilbert, a supporter of Fair Play who had visited Cuba during the Christmas break at the end of 1960, wrote an extensive article describing his experiences and observations about the social and political gains of the Cuban people. By chance Gilbert had visited Playa Girón, where the revolutionary government was focusing development efforts that had already begun transforming conditions of life and work for the impoverished residents of the Zapata Swamp, previously one of the most isolated and backward regions of the country. Little did we know at the time the special significance Playa Girón would have in a matter of weeks, not only for the Cuban people but for the work of supporters of the Cuban Revolution.

The unfolding debate at Carleton, as elsewhere, was deeply affected by hearing accounts in early 1961 of the murder of young literacy campaign workers in Cuba by CIA-financed and -armed counterrevolutionary bands in remote areas. Homilies from liberal opponents of the revolution about the need to see both sides of the story seemed brutally hypocritical beside photos of Cuban teenagers lynched for the crime of teaching peasant families to read and write. Or for the crime of wearing a militia uniform as they walked home at night, unarmed.

Supporters of the revolution also put a spotlight on the unjust and brutal treatment of prorevolutionary Cubans in the United States. Only days before the Bay of Pigs invasion, Francisco Molina, an unemployed Cuban worker who supported the revolution, was convicted in New York City on second-degree murder charges. The *Carletonian* carried the story. Molina had been framed and found guilty of murder for the accidental death of a young Venezuelan girl during a fight, provoked by an assault by Cuban counterrevolutionaries, that broke out in a New York restaurant during Prime Minister Fidel Castro's September 1960 visit to speak before the United Nations General Assembly. On grounds of "national security," the judge prevented Molina's defense attorneys from pursuing the identity and other relevant information about the counterrevolutionary Cubans involved in the incident. As the respectable press howled about the lack of justice in Cuba, the class character of "justice" in the United States could not have been more clearly demonstrated for us.

During these same weeks, a major fight involving much greater forces than those at Carleton alone broke out over campus recognition of the student Fair Play for Cuba Committee. In early February the student government association, by a two-thirds majority, approved an application for recognition from the campus chapter of the FPCC. A very vocal minority objected, arguing that a group avowedly dedicated to "dissemination of material both of fact and opinion on contemporary U.S.-Cuba affairs" and establishing "broader understanding of U.S.-Cuba relations" could not be a legitimate campus organization since, they charged, the FPCC was "vulnerable to communist influence." A cartoon in the following issue of the campus paper lampooned the right-wing arguments; it depicted Nikita Khrushchev, Mao Zedong, and Fidel Castro standing behind *Carletonian* editor John Miller, chortling, "Well, boys, what'll we put in next week's *Carletonian?*"

The large majority vote by the student government association didn't settle the matter, however. A faculty meeting also had to approve the charters of all student organizations before they could be recognized, normally a formality following a favorable student government recommendation. After stalling for a month on technicalities, in mid-March the faculty assembly took up the FPCC application, along with a letter from three students objecting to recognition of the campus chapter. Appended to the letter were excerpts from the records of the Senate Internal Security Subcommittee, chaired by Democratic Party senators James Eastland of Mississippi and Thomas Dodd of Connecticut. The committee was at that time conducting a congressional witch-hunt hearing on "communist influence" in the Fair Play for Cuba Committee.

Dean of the College Richard Gilman told a closed faculty meeting he "had information saying that the Socialist Workers Party have a special and partisan interest in the Fair Play for Cuba Committee—that they are using it for their own purposes." According to the *Carletonian*, "Gilman admitted that this information presented was not documented evidence but rather was the 'opinion' of two sources," whose identity he refused to reveal because of the "nature of the information and the sources."

The campus paper reported that a request from the campus Fair Play organizers that they be given even "one documented incident to indicate use of the FPCC by another political group for purposes other than those enumerated in its charter" was denied. Also rejected was a request that they be provided with the identities of even one of the purported "sources" so they could "confront Fair Play's accusers" and either refute or corroborate their "opinions."

A few days before the faculty vote on recognition, Gilman asked me to drop by his office. He handed me copies of expurgated pages from an FBI file on the Fair Play for Cuba Committee containing informers' reports on meetings of the committee in Minneapolis-St. Paul, including garbled comments attributed to individuals identified as members of the Socialist Workers Party. When the dean asked me if I recognized any of the names, I assured him I did, and that a number of them were my comrades. They were members of the party I was soon to join. I also protested that I knew them well enough to assure him they could not have made the kinds of remarks attributed to them by the FBI's apolitical stooges.

"That really makes no difference, does it Jack?" was Gilman's only reply. It was a very short meeting.

It wasn't the facts or content that mattered, it was the accusation, or rather the threat behind the accusation. That was the message. This was the tried-and-true witch-hunting method machined during the war administration of Franklin Roosevelt, broadened in use by Harry Truman, then honed over more than half a decade in the late 1940s and early 1950s by Richard Nixon, Joseph McCarthy, and their ilk. It was a method still very much in use in 1961. "X" and "Y" were known members of the Socialist Workers Party, a communist organization, and the Socialist Workers Party was on the Attorney General's List of Communist or Subversive Organizations—in those days that was often sufficient to end further discussion.

Even with all this, Gilman wasn't sure enough of a majority to allow a faculty vote on recognition of the Fair Play for Cuba Committee. On March 11 the faculty accepted the dean's recommendation not to act on the student government proposal, pending clarification of some matters about which he was awaiting "further information." Everyone got the point. The school year would soon be over, and the central leaders of the committee were seniors. The dean and others hoped their "problem" would be eliminated before the next academic year began.

But wars register sharpening not diminishing class struggle. Far from disappearing, their "problem" was about to get worse.

■

With the bombing of the Cuban airports on April 15; the April 16 mass mobilization that registered the socialist character of the revolution, politically preparing the Cuban people for the impending invasion; and the April 17 landing of the mercenary forces at the Bay of Pigs followed by their crushing defeat fewer than three days later—all documented by Fidel Castro and José Ramón Fernández in the pages that follow—everything ceased being normal.

One of the routines of campus life at Carleton was the lunchtime reading of the day's news dispatches. In each dormitory dining room, as a sit-down lunch was being served by student waiters working for their scholarship funds, the head waiter would read a handful of the morning's press dispatches from United Press International. UPI's teletype service was provided free of charge by Lucky Strike cigarettes to the campus radio station on condition that Lucky Strike be acknowledged as the sponsor of all news programs. Which it was. Except when "The Sleepy Fox," who hosted the morning wake-up music and news program, sometimes announced the sponsor was a popular brand of Havana cigar. He also prepared students for the day by opening with the "July 26 Hymn," an antidote to "The Star-Spangled Banner" with which radio and

TV stations in the United States signed on and off each broadcast session.

On Monday, April 17, the dry, slightly cynical style of the lunchtime news readings changed. Initial reports of the assault on Cuba were suddenly greeted by slightly flushed right-wingers leading rhythmic chants of "War! War! War!" The rapidity of the transformation, and the incipient violence that lay so close to the surface beneath the "political debate," was something none of us had seen before.

Three days later, for those who had led the chants, the unimaginable had happened. You could almost see the ranks of supporters of Fair Play for Cuba expanding as the news readers flatly intoned UPI dispatches announcing the utter rout of the mercenary forces at "Cochinos Bay." We were surprised as some campus workers, instructors, and students we barely knew—who had remained poker-faced during the previous three days—came up with a handshake or smile to say something friendly, even if not openly mentioning Cuba.

The year 1961 in Cuba was "The Year of Education," when more than 100,000 young people, the big majority of them teenagers, left their homes and spread out across the country to eradicate illiteracy from Cuba before the year was up. In unexpected ways, 1961 was also our year of education.

One of our biggest lessons was what happens in an imperialist country when war begins.

In a matter of hours on April 17, the broad undecided center had shrunk to a voiceless kernel. Months of concentrated political action preparing for the inevitable battle fell into place in a few decisive days. Committed builders of the Fair Play for Cuba Committee at Carleton in early 1961 had been fewer than half a dozen. But now came the payoff for the weeks of education, propaganda work, writing, talking, pushing for and organizing open political debate, and taking up the challenges of every opponent on every issue. As the workers and peasants of Cuba inflicted a crushing defeat on U.S. imperialism, support for the political positions we had been defending exploded overnight. But only because we were there, we were prepared, and we were ready to respond.

The sharp and violent polarization that erupted as the first shots were fired taught us another big lesson. As opponents of the U.S.-sponsored invasion, we were in the streets within hours. But so too were the ultra-right-wing cadres of the Young Americans for Freedom (YAF) who mobilized to try to physically prevent Fair Play for Cuba Committee actions from taking place.

On the steps of the University of Minnesota student union on April 18, where the campus FPCC had called a protest speak-out, a largely hostile crowd of several hundred swelled to well over a thousand as right-wingers pelted the speakers with snowballs and milk cartons, while the cops smiled. With the predominantly liberal and pacifist rally organizers unprepared to defend the meeting, John Greenagle, state chairman of the YAF, forced his way onto the platform to deplore the defeat of Batista, while a few other students appealed for "tolerance" and "dialogue." Even one of those who had been lined up to speak as an opponent of the invasion rushed to take his distance from the Cuban Revolution, bleating out, "We don't support Castro. Once again the Cuban people are under the heel of a dictator, but is an American-supported invasion the way to help them? Is this armed force any better than Batista or Castro?"

An effigy of the "commie" Fair Play for Cuba Committee was hung in front of the chemistry building the next morning.

Similar confrontations took place at other schools across the United States, from Madison, Wisconsin, to Providence, Rhode Island.

We learned in practice what Batista and the Cuban Revolution had already taught us from afar: that in the United States, too, we would have to defeat the reactionary thugs in the streets even to have the right to make our positions known.

We got an education in liberalism, too, as most of our faculty friends went silent or absented themselves, rather than take on a dean (a reserved and tolerant one, no less) suddenly waving the Attorney General's list and FBI informer reports in their faces. A couple of prominent faculty conservatives, in fact, were more steadfast in their defense of our rights than were most of their liberal colleagues.

We saw student allies who had previously been staunch defenders of the Cuban Revolution, or at least of Fair Play's right to function like other campus organizations, suddenly develop cold feet; they were discovering that future career plans were incompatible with continued association with friends who were becoming communists.

Others made the opposite life decisions in a matter of days.

Our understanding of these class questions was accelerated immeasurably by the fact we were sharing our day-by-day experiences, as well as talking about them into the wee hours of the night with communist workers in the Twin Cities. They were people like V.R. Dunne, who had been a member of the Communist International from its founding in 1919, a leader of the Teamsters strikes and organizing drives in the Upper Midwest during the 1930s, and one of the first victims railroaded to prison by the federal government under the infamous Smith "Gag" Act for opposition to U.S. imperialism leading up to and during World War II.

These workers pointed us to the history of the class struggle in the United States, to the lessons we needed to learn from the workers and farmers whose fighting legacy we inherited here. They drew on this rich history to help us understand what we had to be prepared for as we went up against the most violent and brutal ruling class in the world.

Above all, they taught those of us who, like themselves, were so strongly and passionately attracted to the example being set by the fighting workers and peasants of Cuba that the challenge—*for us*—was not there. Cuba's workers and farmers had proven they could take care of themselves. They helped us see that our fight was in the United States. That Washington, to paraphrase Cuban Division General Enrique Carreras, would never be able to get that bone out of its throat.

Those workers like Dunne and others helped us see that the

contest would end only with the defeat of the revolution in Cuba or a victorious socialist revolution in the United States.

"There is one thing we can most certainly tell Mr. Kennedy," Fidel Castro told a cheering crowd in Cuba on March 13 of that year. "A victorious revolution will be seen in the United States before a victorious counterrevolution in Cuba."

That had become our conviction too. As beyond belief as this appeared to the average American, it had become clear to us it was the only *realistic* perspective, and we set out to speed the day.

The continual interchange between new, young activists, mostly on the campuses, and communist workers whose experiences on the job and in the unions over these days paralleled ours as we all went through the same rapid political shifts and changes, helped deepen our understanding of what we were living through. Our rail worker comrades reported receiving a friendly nod from fellow workers for telling the truth about Cuba in the same way that we were being encouraged in many indirect ways by those on campus we had not previously realized were following so closely what we were saying and doing.

We came to appreciate that everything depended on having done the political work beforehand. We learned firsthand how dangerously wrong and class-biased were the fears and semi-hysterical reactions of many of our campus-based colleagues. The source of reaction was not "backward American workers" but the U.S. ruling class, and the semihysterical middle-class layers who served as their transmission belt. The danger came also from those who, whether they owned up to it or not, had set out on a life course to camouflage, help divert attention from, and politically rationalize the rapacious and brutal actions of that ruling class. The battle before us was first of all a political battle inside the working class, as part of the working class.

■

As Cuban workers and farmers pressed forward their socialist revolution and U.S. aggression mounted in reaction to their gains, the lessons transformed the way we looked at the battle for Black rights in the United States as well. The mass proletarian struggle to bring down the Jim Crow system of statutory segregation throughout the South, with its various forms of discrimination extending throughout the country, was marching toward bloody victories at the same time that the Cuban Revolution was advancing. We could see in practice that there were powerful social forces within the United States capable of carrying out a revolutionary social transformation like the working people of Cuba were bringing into being.

The core of the activists defending the Cuban Revolution were young people who had cut their political eyeteeth as part of the civil rights battles, supporting the Woolworth lunch counter sit-ins and joining or supporting marches and other protests in Alabama, Georgia, Mississippi, and elsewhere in the South.

The many faces of reaction, some in Ku Klux Klan hoods, others with sheriff's uniforms and FBI jackets protecting them; the lynchings and murders on isolated country roads; the dogs and water cannons unleashed on protesters—all were burned in our consciousness as part of the lessons we were learning about the violence and brutality of the U.S. ruling class and the lengths to which it will go to defend its property and prerogatives.

And we were learning lessons, too, from the armed self-defense organized by Black veterans in Monroe, North Carolina, and elsewhere in the South. Immediately following the U.S. defeat at the Bay of Pigs, during a debate in the Political Committee of the United Nations General Assembly, Cuban Foreign Minister Raúl Roa read a message that former Monroe NAACP president Robert F. Williams had asked him to convey to the U.S. government.

"Now that the United States has proclaimed military support for people willing to rebel against oppression," Williams wrote, "oppressed Negroes in the South urgently request tanks, artillery, bombs, money, use of American air fields and white mercenaries to crush racist tyrants who have betrayed the American Revolution and Civil War."

We rapidly came to see that the legal and extralegal violence directed against those fighting for their rights and dignity as human beings here in the United States was one and the same as the mounting overt and covert aggression against the people of Cuba. We placed the struggle for Black rights in the world. It became totally intertwined for us with the stakes in defending the Cuban Revolution.

This was exemplified above all by the convergence of the Cuban Revolution and Malcolm X, whose voice of uncompromising revolutionary struggle—by any means necessary—was then increasingly making itself heard. Malcolm welcomed Fidel Castro to the Hotel Theresa in Harlem during the Cuban delegation's trip to the United Nations in 1960. Malcolm invited Che Guevara to address a meeting of the Organization of Afro-American Unity during Che's trip to New York in 1964.

For us, these and other expressions of the growing mutual respect and solidarity that marked relations between Malcolm X and the Cuban leadership were further confirmation of our own developing world view.

■

The April 1961 actions condemning the U.S.-organized invasion of Cuba—held in a score of cities across the United States, as well as a number of small college towns—registered an important moment in U.S. politics in another regard.

In many cities, for the first time in decades, these were united front actions, called under the banner of the Fair Play for Cuba Committee and organized both by those identified with the *Militant* newspaper and by those who looked for leadership to the *Daily Worker*, newspaper of the Communist Party. Representatives of each of these historic currents in the broad working-class movement joined July 26 Movement speakers and prominent individuals not affiliated with any current on speak-

AP / WIDE WORLD PHOTOS

MILITANT

"We came to see that the legal and extralegal violence directed against those fighting for their dignity as human beings here in the United States was one and the same as the mounting aggression against the people of Cuba. The struggle for Black rights became totally intertwined for us with the stakes in defending the Cuban Revolution."

Top: Young demonstrators protest cop killing of 19-year-old Timothy Thomas, Cincinnati, April 2001. **Bottom:** Neighbor explains events surrounding the killing to Cuban youth leaders Yanelis Martínez and Javier Dueñas (right) at the place where the shooting occurred.

ers' platforms from New York to Detroit, from Minneapolis to San Francisco. The actions were testimony to the impact of the Cuban Revolution as well as the leadership of the July 26 Movement.

The potential for unified actions had received a boost during the summer of 1960 when scores of young people from the United States, affiliated and unaffiliated, traveled to Cuba, many of us participating in the July 26 celebration in the Sierra Maestra mountains and attending the First Latin American Youth Congress in Havana. We took part in the wide-ranging political debate among young people from all over the Americas and the world, trying to understand the onrushing struggle we were part of and thinking through the questions addressed by Che Guevara in his opening speech to the youth congress, where he asked: "Is this revolution communist?"

The answer Guevara gave posed the issues we were all discussing. "After the usual explanation as to what communism is (I leave aside the hackneyed accusations by imperialism and the colonial powers, who confuse everything)," Guevara responded, "I would answer that if this revolution is Marxist— and listen well that I say 'Marxist'—it is because it discovered, by its own methods, the road pointed out by Marx."

Guevara's explanation coincided well with the conclusions I was groping toward during that decisive summer, when all the major imperialist-owned industries in Cuba were nationalized by massive mobilizations of working people from one end of the island to the other. Guevara's view was far from a unanimous one, however, either in Cuba or among the young people from across the Americas who had flocked to Cuba. We spent many long hours there debating among ourselves the political and theoretical issues that were posed.

Despite sharp political differences over the dynamic of the revolution in Cuba and class politics in the United States, the fact that different currents were able to come together in action against the U.S. government, even if briefly, registered the weight of the Cuban Revolution in the Americas, and the degree to which it opened the road to shatter old molds and alter the relationship of class forces that had for years dominated what was broadly considered the "left."

■

The campus Fair Play for Cuba Committees and the actions in response to the U.S.-sponsored invasion at the Bay of Pigs also dealt one of the first blows to anticommunist witch-hunting and red-baiting. As the Carleton example illustrated, the hearings of the Senate Internal Security Subcommittee aimed at dividing and destroying the effectiveness of Fair Play simply failed to have the same effect on students they would have had several years earlier.

Throughout these same months of intense political action in defense of Cuba, Committees to Abolish HUAC, the House Un-American Activities Committee, had been mushrooming on campuses across the country. On April 21, one day after a Union Square demonstration of 5,000 in New York City condemning the invasion of Cuba, nearly the same number turned out in the city for an anti-HUAC rally to protest the imminent jailing of several prominent civil liberties and civil rights activists for refusing to cooperate with the House committee.

Among students, especially, conviction that the U.S. rulers were lying about Washington's total control of the invasion and other actions against Cuba went hand in hand with rejection of the government's witch-hunt methods. Openness to searching for the truth about Cuba was incompatible with a belief that the opinions of some should not be heard because they were communists or were labeled communists.

In a prelude to what happened during the opening years of the anti–Vietnam War movement in the mid- and late 1960s, the witch-hunting moves of right-wing students and faculty, far from paralyzing organizing efforts, became targets of derision and scorn. The majority of students awakening to political life simply refused to support attempts to exclude members and supporters of the Socialist Workers Party and Communist Party, or any other group, from the Fair Play for Cuba Committee.

■

The victory at Playa Girón punctured the myth of U.S. imperialism's invincibility. It left us with the conviction that the Cuban Revolution would be at the center of the class struggle inside the United States as long as the working class was in power in Cuba, and we had become convinced that such would be the case for the rest of our lives. The U.S. rulers could never accept revolutionary Cuba and would never stop trying to get rid of it and the example it set. Their most vital class interests were at stake. That was the truth we had to bring to working people in the United States and prepare to act on.

Within days of the Bay of Pigs defeat, President Kennedy stepped up covert operations against Cuba and began organizing directly from the White House even more extensive sabotage missions, assassination attempts, and military preparations for a U.S. invasion. We didn't know the scope of those operations at the time, nor that the administration only a year and a half later would push them to the brink of unleashing a nuclear war. But we did know that Fidel Castro was speaking the truth to the people of Cuba and the world in his April 23 report on the victory at Playa Girón when he emphasized that the victory "does not mean that the danger is past. Quite the contrary. We believe that the danger is now great, above all, the danger of direct aggression by the United States."

The victory of Cuban working people at Playa Girón, together with the concentrated class-struggle experience we had gained over a few months of intense action, had in a matter of a few days transformed a group of young people for the rest of our lives. Before the Bay of Pigs there had been only one member of the Young Socialist Alliance at Carleton College, myself, and one at the University of Minnesota, John Chelstrom, an eighteen-year-old freshman who, when everyone else froze in front of the rabidly hostile crowd, stepped forward and led off the April 18 speak-out on the steps of the student union, not only opposing the invasion but openly identifying himself with the Cuban Revolution.

Between those days of concentrated politics, and similar experiences lived through during the October 1962 "Missile" Crisis, we recruited scores of young people who were won to the communist movement not for months or years, but for life. At Carleton College alone during that brief span, these recruits included over a dozen who later became leaders of the communist movement—national officers of the Young Socialist Alliance, national officers and National Committee members of the Socialist Workers Party, editors of the *Young Socialist*, the *Militant*, the *New International*, leaders of the movement's industrial trade union work, and of countless defense committees and coalitions, editors of Pathfinder Press—individuals who to this day remain committed to the communist movement and active along the political course they were won to in those decisive days. In fact, forty years later, a large majority of them were involved in bringing this book into print!

Through those experiences four decades ago, we were won not primarily to an ideological position or even a moral stance, but to a course of political conduct and, most importantly, to the habits consistent with it. With a sense of history, we signed on for the duration, recognizing that the revolutionary fight for power, while an international struggle, can only be waged country by country, and possibly the most satisfying victory of all will be in the United States. For us, what Cuban workers and peasants had accomplished was the example in our own political lifetime of the necessity and the possibility of revolution, of how to fight to win, of the capacity of ordinary human beings to transform themselves as they confront challenges and take on responsibilities they would have previously deemed impossible.

We and millions like us were the only ones who could "remove the bone." To do so we would have to follow the example of the Rebel Army in Cuba, whose struggle culminated in a nationwide insurrection in 1959 and soon established a workers and farmers government. We would have to follow the example the revolutionary militias, police, and army had set in smashing the invasion at the Bay of Pigs.

■

The pages that follow are not solely a celebration of the victory at Playa Girón on the occasion of its fortieth anniversary. Rather, in clear and unambiguous words, these pages register accurately the historical accomplishments achieved there.

The July 1999 testimony offered by José Ramón Fernández draws its unusual power not only from being the firsthand account of the field commander of the main column that fought and defeated the U.S.-organized invasion, but also from his use of the major accounts published by those who recruited, trained, and commanded the enemy forces. He points not only to what the revolutionary leadership of Cuba knew and did at the time, guaranteeing the decisive victory at Playa Girón. Fernández also cites the judgments and opinions rendered in the maps and charts the mercenary forces later drew for themselves, as well as the balance sheets of top CIA officials during the months and years that followed their totally unexpected defeat.

The three speeches by Cuban commander in chief Fidel Castro excerpted here capture the intensity of the moment, the stakes for the people of Cuba, and their confidence in ultimate victory. The same is true of the April 15 calls to battle by Raúl Castro and Che Guevara, as well as the war communiqués issued by the revolutionary government between April 17 and the victory on April 19. The confidence marking each of them is born not of some unfounded belief in military invincibility, but of the recognition that history and justice are on their side, and that the price the empire will have to pay to conquer them is one no capitalist politician will be capable of doing or willing to try.

The U.S. rulers, and those who follow their lead, still to this day cannot grasp what Fidel Castro stressed in his April 23 report to the Cuban people on the victory at Playa Girón, and what José Ramón Fernández underlines in his testimony: that the military strategy and tactics of those who planned the invasion at the Bay of Pigs were sound; the defeat was rooted in their class blindness to what the men and women of Cuba had wrought, to the *objective* power of a just cause and of an armed and revolutionary people committed to defend it and acting with the decisiveness and speed necessary to shape the course of history.

The invading forces lost their will to fight before they ran out of bullets. During three days of battle, they could never even get off the beaches, and additional U.S. air or naval support would have made no difference to the ultimate outcome.

Most importantly, for those of us living and working in the United States, this is a book about the future of the class struggle here. It is about the workers and farmers in the imperialist heartland, and the youth who are attracted to the line of march of these toilers—workers and farmers whose revolutionary capacities are today as utterly discounted by the ruling powers as were those of the peasant and proletarian masses of Cuba. And just as wrongly.

Cuba's victory at Playa Girón registered the first great defeat of U.S. imperialism in the Americas. It will not be the last.

That will occur right here.

'There will be a victorious revolution in the United States before a victorious counterrevolution in Cuba'

IN SEPTEMBER 1960, addressing the United Nations General Assembly, Cuban prime minister Fidel Castro announced to the world: "In the coming year, our country intends to wage its great battle against illiteracy, with the ambitious goal of teaching every single illiterate person in the country"—one million Cubans, roughly one-third of the adult population—"to read and write." And that's exactly what they did, as some 100,000 young people, most of them teenagers, went to the countryside and lived and worked alongside peasant families.

Today we are celebrating the fortieth anniversary of that historic conquest.

On April 15, 1961, when the Yankee-organized mercenaries announced their imminent invasion by simultaneously bombing three Cuban airfields, the revolutionary government mobilized the people's militias and other military units. In the declaration announcing that state of alert, Fidel Castro called on all Cubans to "occupy their assigned posts, whether in a military unit or a workplace"—and he added, in the same sentence, "with

Based on a talk presented March 18, 2001, in Seattle, Washington, and March 11 in New York City to some 450 participants in meetings celebrating the fortieth anniversary of Cuba's successful campaign to wipe out illiteracy and the victory of the Cuban people over Washington's mercenary army at the Bay of Pigs.

47

no interruption in production, the literacy campaign, or a single revolutionary task."

Four days later, when the counterrevolutionary forces had been defeated, the communiqué signed by Fidel reporting that victory to the Cuban people was demonstratively dated: "April 19, 1961, Year of Education."

You can find both documents in the new Pathfinder book, *Playa Girón/Bay of Pigs: Washington's First Military Defeat in the Americas*, whose publication in English and Spanish we are also celebrating here today.

Nineteen sixty-one in Cuba was the Year of Education in all the meanings of that word—the capacity to learn, to produce, to become a more disciplined revolutionary soldier, to create, to develop. The Year of Education meant making culture more accessible. It meant bravery in serving the highest human goals. It meant extending a hand of solidarity to anyone fighting against injustice and oppression anywhere in the world. It meant offering your life to achieve these goals.

Fidel Castro, Ernesto Che Guevara, and other leaders of the Cuban Revolution were very much aware that the greatest obstacle to the line of march of the toilers is the tendency, promoted and perpetuated by the exploiting classes, for working people to underestimate ourselves, to underestimate what we can accomplish, to doubt our own worth. That's why revolutionists in Cuba were so proud that the literacy effort had continued with minimal disruption as the battle against the invaders—a battle for the very life of the revolution—was fought and won. "The literacy campaign has not stopped even during these days," announced Fidel Castro in his April 23 report on the victory to the Cuban people.

Whatever any particular individual was doing over those three days, April 17–19—whether deployed at the front, working in the fields or factories, or helping someone learn to read and write—the Cuban people felt the bond of a common battle waged by equals. A common bond that provided a basis for discipline, a basis for the shared joy of construction, the joy of creation, and the joy of victory in battle over those who sought to destroy everything their revolution was making possible.

What a moment for the people of Cuba to announce to the world the socialist character of the revolution!

A little more than a year later Che Guevara told the congress of the Union of Young Communists (UJC)—in a speech you can find in Pathfinder's *Che Guevara Talks to Young People*—that young communists had the responsibility to be "the first in work, the first in study, the first in defense of the country." And he congratulated them for the three words they had put on the emblem of their organization—study, work, and rifle.

These are the emblems of all Cubans, Che said, permanent emblems, not just momentary ones.

The rifle, because no progress toward the liberation of toiling humanity is secure unless the exploiting classes know we are ready to defend those gains by any means necessary. That was the truth confirmed once again at Playa Girón and soon retested and reconfirmed during the October 1962 "Missile" Crisis.

Work, often depicted by a shovel or a machete, because the transformation of nature by human labor, social labor, is not only the source of all wealth but the foundation for all culture. Without the shovel and machete, there's nothing for the rifle to defend.

And study, depicted by a pencil, a symbol of the literacy campaign, because the capacity to read and write gives access to the cumulative conquests of all previous human endeavor and opens the doors to workers and farmers to participate as equals in every aspect of social and political life. It makes them better able to transform production and the conditions of life and work, better able to take control of their own destiny.

The literacy campaign was central to strengthening the worker-peasant alliance on which revolutionary Cuba was founded; it was central to narrowing the gulf between toilers in city and countryside. Peasants and their families in prerevolutionary Cuba had virtually no educational opportunities. This was especially true for women in rural areas. So the literacy campaign struck a mighty blow for the emancipation of women, too.

A central part of the education of every revolutionary-minded person is coming to recognize the terror, violence, and degradation on which the landlords and capitalists base their rule. That's one of the lessons underlined by José Ramón Fernández, commander of the main column that repelled the invaders at Playa Girón, in his July 1999 testimony before a Havana court during the trial of a lawsuit brought by the people of Cuba against the U.S. government for the thousands of deaths and massive physical destruction Washington's decades-long effort to destroy the Cuban Revolution has wrought.

In 1961 the literacy campaign volunteers were among those in Cuba against whom the U.S. government unleashed its counterrevolutionary assassins and torturers. As we explained in the foreword to *Playa Girón*, for young people in the United States during those opening years of the revolution, the press dispatches and photographs depicting "Cuban teenagers lynched for the crime of teaching peasant families to read and write" offered a graphic representation of the motives, the real character of the contending class forces confronting each other not just in Cuba but the world over.

Such images confirmed what young people in the United States in the early 1960s were learning here at home about the lynchings, night-riding terror, and police violence, both local and federal, against Blacks and civil rights fighters. This helped us understand the class reality that cop beatings, frame-ups, humiliations, and, yes, executions on the streets are part of the everyday life of millions of workers—daily horrors that bear down disproportionately on Blacks, Chicanos, Puerto Ricans, and other oppressed nationalities. It opened our eyes slowly but surely to recognize that the capitalist rulers will unleash fascist terror in face of a challenge to their rule by workers and farmers.

■

The victory at Playa Girón reminds us of the price toilers must be ready to pay to win our freedom from exploitation and oppression and then to defend it. We can't help but be affected by the fearlessness displayed by tens of thousands of Cuban workers and peasants, many of them very young—by their courage and determination in face of death. That's one of the qualities of a people engaged in a profound revolutionary transformation of their circumstances and themselves.

What's so striking about Cuban revolutionists, however, is not their courage and determination in face of death. *It's their attitude toward life*. That, above all, is what the élan, the discipline, the bravery that ensured the triumph at Playa Girón were all about.

That's why, as José Ramón Fernández says in his testimony, there was such surprise in Washington in April 1961 "at the scope of the Cuban people's victory." The outcome, he points out, "can be explained only by the courage of a people who saw the January 1 [1959] triumph as the genuine opportunity to determine their own future. This is why they proudly wore the militia uniforms and were on alert, and willing to fight, with the firm conviction they would win."

That's what the U.S. rulers did not understand—and even more importantly, *can never understand*. They do not and cannot understand the scope of the capacities of workers and farmers engaged in struggle, *revolutionary* struggle above all. They cannot understand human beings like the militia members in that wonderful photograph the *Militant* newspaper ran this week of the First Company of the 134th Battalion celebrating their victory at Playa Girón.

If this weren't true—if the ruling class could understand what propels workers and farmers into revolutionary action; if they understood what we are ready to fight and die for, or could *learn* to understand it—then socialist revolution would be an illusion. But they do not and cannot.

In order to rationalize the legitimacy of their exploitative system before the eyes of society as a whole, the rulers rely on *ideology*. Contrary to the bourgeoisie's pretensions to civilization and culture, there are no "great ideas" or scientific social theories whose inexorable conclusion is that a handful of property-holding families must forever grow wealthy off the labor of the majority of humanity, maintaining their class dictatorship by whatever force and violence is necessary. That's not a law of nature, or of political economy.

The capitalists in the United States are particularly pragmatic. They have no theories or ideas. They just do what they must to maintain their class rule, and then promote ideological justifications for it. They market these as buzzwords, hack phrases, and coarse Americanism, through "news" shows, "news" analyses, "newspapers," and talk radio and TV.

But bourgeois ideology is not a conspiracy. It's not some clever plot they hatch. The closer the rulers' rationalizations come to something with a family resemblance to social thought, the more impossible it becomes for them and their children to disentangle what they, as a class, *want* and *claim* to be true from the truth itself. The same ideological illusions hold sway among the middle-class and professional layers who look to the bourgeois rulers and act on their behalf.

In *Capital*, in the chapter called "The Fetishism of the Commodity and Its Secret," Karl Marx observes that the very foundation of capitalist social relations—the fact that all profits originate from the exchange of commodities whose value is solely the creation of human labor—is camouflaged behind what goes by the name of "economics," but is in fact vulgar apologetics for bourgeois rule. But these ideological self-rationalizations are believed by the capitalists and those they hire to propagate them, Marx says.

"These formulas," Marx writes, "which bear the unmistakable stamp of belonging to a social formation in which the process of production has mastery over man, instead of the opposite, appear to the political economists' bourgeois consciousness to be as much a self-evident and nature-imposed necessity as productive labour itself."

Because the bourgeoisie and their servants believe their own ideology, they end up making political misjudgments about the capacities of working people—about the toilers whose courageous actions allow them to begin escaping the domination of these ghosts. At decisive moments, the rulers make big miscalculations. That's why, in the end, they will lose.

Over the years, I've frequently heard the question: "Didn't most top CIA and White House officials really know there would be no uprising by the Cuban people in response to the Bay of Pigs invasion?" The answer is, no. It's not that simple. And it's worth taking a few minutes to discuss why.

A good place to start is the judgment by José Ramón Fernández that "from a strategic and tactical point of view, the enemy's idea was well-conceived." We should take that assessment as dead serious. But it contradicts all the most common evaluations promoted for forty years by the U.S. rulers and their propagandists to rationalize Cuba's stunning victory. They point to the CIA's supposed blunders, or to Kennedy's claimed vacillations, or to a combination of both.

Fernández rejects this. "The mercenaries came well organized, well armed, and well supported," he says. "What they lacked was a just cause to defend. That is why they did not fight with the same passion, courage, conviction, valor, firmness, bravery, and spirit of victory as did the revolutionary forces."

Che Guevara made the same point just a few weeks after the victory at Playa Girón. It's in a talk he gave on May 8 to a gathering of electrical workers and militia members in Havana. I read it on the plane flying out here from New York. The *Militant* is planning to run the talk as a feature in the April 2 issue. Don't miss it; it's pure pleasure.

The U.S. government's "operation was well conceived from a military point of view," Che said. "They did their mathematical calculations as if they were confronting the German army and coming to take a beachhead at Normandy." They organized the invasion at the Bay of Pigs "with the efficiency they display in such matters."

"But they failed to measure the moral relationship of forces," Che added. "First, they mismeasured our ability to react, including not only our ability to react in face of aggression, our ability to react in the face of a danger, and to mobilize our forces and send them to the site of the battle—they mismeasured that. But they were also wrong in measuring the fighting capacity of the opposing sides."

The U.S. rulers, Che said, figured they needed only 1,000 men to carry out a successful invasion and hold a beachhead in Cuba. "But they needed 1,000 men there who would fight to the death," he emphasized, and that they did not have. "Someone whose daddy had 30,000 acres of land, and who comes here solely to show his presence so the 30,000 acres of land will be returned to him—you can't ask him to die at the hand of a peasant who had nothing and who has a ferocious desire to kill him because they're coming to take the peasant's land away."

"They have always been wrong about us," Che concluded. "They have always arrived late. And they have never done anything that did not serve instead to strengthen the trust of the people in their government, to make the revolution more militant: in short, to strengthen us more."

The U.S. rulers *were* wrong about the workers and farmers of Cuba. Officials in the CIA and White House expected the invasion force, after a few days, to spark some uprisings against the revolutionary government. They anticipated some divisions among the officers of Cuba's armed forces, too. By analogy, the imperialists saw the government in Cuba as some tropical variety of a Stalinist regime, with the same inherent brittleness. And they saw the cadres of the Revolutionary Armed Forces as some radical variant of a bourgeois Latin American officer corps, comparable to those they had long been used to dealing with.

Up until just five weeks before the invasion, the CIA's plan had been for the mercenary brigade to land near the city of Trinidad. Trinidad lies at the foot of the Escambray mountains, where counterrevolutionary bands had been most active. A CIA memo assured the Kennedy administration that a relatively large and determined invasion force in that area would, "it is hoped, demoralize the militia and induce defections . . . impair the

Top: Thousands of young literacy brigade volunteers joined December 1961 "Rally of the pencils" in Havana to celebrate successful completion of year-long campaign to teach almost one million peasants and workers to read and write. **Bottom:** April 1961 speakout at University of Minnesota against U.S.-organized Bay of Pigs invasion was met by hostile crowd, a small core of whom pelted speakers with snowballs and milk cartons. Young supporters of revolutionary Cuba learned how to defend their right to organize at the same time as they rebutted the arguments of enemies of the revolution.

"1961 was Cuba's Year of Education, when 100,000 young people spread out across the country to eradicate illiteracy. 1961 was also our year of education."

"What's striking about Cuban revolutionists is not their courage and determination in face of death. It's their attitude toward life."

LEE LOCKWOOD

During 1956–58 revolutionary war in Cuba, young combatants who volunteered for the most difficult and hazardous assignments proudly took the name, "Suicide Squad" **(pictured at top)**. In the words of Che Guevara, these soldiers served as an "example of revolutionary morale" for the entire Rebel Army. They set an example of discipline, selfless courage, and joie de vivre for youth the world over.
Left: On January 1, 1959, Cuban working people in Havana took to the streets to ensure victory of the revolution and celebrate fall of U.S.-backed Batista regime.

With the working class in power, the creative potential of labor began being mobilized to meet social needs and transform social relations. **Above:** Volunteer work brigade constructs housing in countryside, 1960. **Top:** May Day rally in Havana, less than two weeks after 1961 Playa Girón victory. With characteristic humor, Cuban workers carry effigy of captured mercenary who had haunted the exclusive social clubs of prerevolutionary Cuba. "He belonged to the Yacht Club. He came and he stayed," the sign reads — echoing Fidel Castro's warning to any would-be invaders: "If they come, they stay!"

"The mass proletarian struggle to bring down Jim Crow segregation in the South, and the forms of discrimination it reinforced throughout the country, was marching toward bloody victories as the Cuban Revolution advanced. We could see in practice that there were powerful social forces in the U.S. capable of carrying out a revolutionary social transformation like working people in Cuba were doing."

CHARLES MOORE / BLACK STAR

Top: Cops in Alabama sic attack dogs on militants defending Black rights during "Battle of Birmingham," April 1963. **Below:** Civil rights demonstrators arrested and held behind jail in Albany, Georgia, July 1962.

Bottom: Crowd waving Cuban flags outside Hotel Theresa in Harlem greets government delegation from Cuba, September 1960, when Fidel Castro addressed United Nations. **Top:** During trip, Castro was welcomed by Malcolm X. Malcolm's "uncompromising revolutionary stance increasingly converged with the course of the Cuban Revolution."

"There will be a victorious revolution in the United States before a victorious counterrevolution in Cuba."

FIDEL CASTRO, MARCH 1961

Top: Strikers confront cops and special deputies during 1934 Minneapolis Teamsters strike. Through this and other hard-fought labor organizing battles in the 1930s, a class-struggle leadership of the Teamsters was forged in the Upper Midwest. It charted a political course independent of the capitalist exploiters and their parties and against their march toward fascism and imperialist war. **Bottom:** Teamsters Local 544 Union Defense Guard, 1938, was formed to meet growing threats by employer-financed fascist forces in Minnesota.

MILITANT

"We were learning lessons about the brutality of the U.S. ruling class and the lengths to which it will go to defend its property and prerogatives. And we were learning lessons, too, from the armed self-defense organized by Black army veterans such as those in Monroe, North Carolina." The Monroe self-defense units that beat back Ku Klux Klan terror **(top)** were organized by Robert F. Williams **(bottom)**, president of the local NAACP chapter and later a leader of the Fair Play for Cuba Committee.

"In a prelude to what happened with the anti–Vietnam War movement, government witch-hunting operations, far from paralyzing student organizing efforts, became targets of derision and scorn."

Facing page: Cops turned waterhoses on demonstration of 5,000 students at San Francisco City Hall, May 13, 1960, protesting hearings by the House Un-American Activities Committee (HUAC). Demonstrators were dragged away and arrested on City Hall steps.

Above: 500 students at Los Angeles City College in 1964 listen to Tom Morgan, one of three Young Socialist Alliance members framed on sedition charges. During the October 1962 Cuban "Missile" Crisis, YSA members at the University of Indiana in Bloomington had helped organize a speak-out against U.S. war moves. A large hostile crowd confronted the protesters, and several were attacked by rightist thugs. A few months later, based solely on a speech at a YSA-sponsored public meeting on campus, Morgan and two others YSAers were indicted for advocating the violent overthrow of the government of the State of Indiana. The YSA helped lead a successful defense campaign that dealt a further blow to witch-hunting. **Bottom:** Anti–Vietnam War demonstration of some 15,000 in San Francisco, October 12, 1968. The march was led by a contingent of 500 active-duty GIs shown here.

"If this revolution is Marxist, it is because it discovered, by its own methods, the road pointed out by Marx."

CHE GUEVARA, JULY 1960

OSVALDO SALAS

LEE LOCKWOOD

Facing page, top: Che Guevara presents opening speech to First Latin American Youth Congress in Havana, July 1960. As congress participants joined popular mobilizations that summer expropriating imperialist-owned industries, young people from across the Americas and the world spent many hours debating the political and theoretical issues posed by the Cuban Revolution. **Facing page, bottom:** The youth congress was inaugurated at Cuba's July 26, 1960, national celebration held in the Sierra Maestra mountains, shown here as thousands made their way to the site.

Youth in the U.S. attracted to Cuban Revolution gave a boost to potential for united actions when Yankee-organized mercenaries invaded at Bay of Pigs. **This page, top:** April 20, 1961, New York City demonstration in response to Bay of Pigs invasion demands, "U.S. Hands Off Cuba!" **This page, bottom:** Three U.S. youth who were among those at the congress (at center, from left), Arnie Kessler, Jack Barnes, and Fred Sweet, pictured here with Cuban militia member Juan González Díaz (at left); the photographer, George Tselos, was a fourth.

"The revolutionary capacities of workers and farmers in the imperialist heartland are today as utterly discounted by the ruling powers as were those of the peasant and proletarian masses of Cuba. And just as wrongly."

Top left: Striking coal miners hold rally in New Mexico at Chevron-owned McKinley mine on Navajo Nation, June 2000. **Bottom left:** Angry crowd jams city council chambers April 2001 in Cincinnati, Ohio, to protest cop killing of 19-year-old Timothy Thomas—the 15th Black man killed by the city's police since 1995.
Top right: Cops attack hundreds of union dock workers in Charleston, South Carolina, January 20, 2000, who were protesting the unloading of a cargo ship by nonunion workers. The action came days after a march of 50,000 against the flying of the Confederate battle flag over the state legislature. **Bottom right:** Somali-born workers, members of the Hotel Employees and Restaurant Employees Union, picket in Minneapolis during successful June 2000 strike.

"The workers, farmers, and exploited toilers of all countries share the same class enemies: the imperialist ruling classes, and the domestic landlords and capitalists dominated by imperialism. That's the only 'we' and 'they' that has any meaning for working people."

M. DESPOTOVIC

T. J. FIGUEROA / MILITANT

Top left: Farmers in Bogor, Indonesia, September 1998, demand land.
Bottom left: Thousands of working people protest government "austerity" policies in Quito, Ecuador, January 2000. The protesters, most of them from the country's indigenous peoples, occupied the Congress and toppled the government.

Top right: The DIN cigarette factory in Nis, Yugoslavia, after one of daily bombings by U.S. planes during 87-day war in 1999. **Bottom right:** Cuban volunteer doctors in South Africa, 2000.

Members of First Company of 134th Militia Battalion celebrate victory at Playa Girón, April 1961. **Left:** Headline of the socialist newsweekly, the *Militant* in response to the Bay of Pigs invasion. The revolutionary example set by Cuban workers and peasants helped win many U.S. youth to the Young Socialist Alliance, to march, fight, study, and work in the vanguard of the working-class movement—for a lifetime.

"Through those days of concentrated politics culminating in the victory at Playa Girón, a layer of young people in the United States were won not primarily to an ideological position or even a moral stance, but to a course of political conduct and, most importantly, to the habits consistent with it. With a sense of history, we signed on for the duration."

morale of the Castro regime, and induce widespread rebellion. If the initial actions proved to be unsuccessful in thus detonating a major revolt, the assault force would retreat to the contiguous mountain area and continue operations as a powerful guerrilla force."

But Kennedy scotched the Trinidad plan on March 11 and insisted that the CIA come up with an alternative. An invasion near a city with a substantial population was too risky politically. The hopes for a rapid uprising were offset by the possibility of an even more stunning defeat. What's more, 40,000 members of Cuba's revolutionary militia had recently completed a successful "cleanup" operation in the Escambray that had greatly diminished the numbers and latitude of the counterrevolutionary bands that might otherwise have been called on by the mercenaries for help.

That's when the invasion site was switched to the Zapata Swamp area near the Bay of Pigs. The plan then became to land on a sparsely populated stretch of beach, win the initial battles, make some progress in gaining popular support, foment divisions, and declare a provisional government. If that proved unsuccessful, then the invasion force was expected to at least hold the beachhead and airfield long enough for diplomatic recognition to be extended and to call for support from the Organization of American States, under cover of which the U.S. government and its closest Latin American allies could intervene.

Meanwhile, the urgency in the Kennedy administration to take action was being ratcheted up by CIA reports that Cuba's revolutionary government and armed people were growing stronger. As one agency memorandum put it, time was not on Washington's side. So with each passing day the White House pressed forward its plans, making constant alterations.

It reminds us of the story about William Randolph Hearst, the jingoist owner of the New York daily *Journal*. Toward the close of Cuba's 1895–98 second war of independence from Spain, Hearst started angling for a pretext to justify Washington's entry into the conflict in order to establish U.S. colonial domination over Cuba. He sent reporters, artists, and photographers to Cuba to cover it. When one of them wired back a cable saying, "There is no war. Request to be recalled," Hearst shot off the reply: "Please remain. You furnish the pictures, I'll furnish the war."

Shortly afterwards, on February 15, 1898, the USS *Maine* exploded under mysterious circumstances in Havana Harbor, and Hearst led the charge with screaming headlines and pages of coverage calling on the people of the United States to "Remember the *Maine*! To hell with Spain." By April Washington had declared war on Madrid, launching the so-called Spanish-American War, which Lenin pointed out was the first war of the imperialist epoch.

Some sixty years later, shortly before midnight on April 16, 1961, the Kennedy administration ordered ashore the initial landing party of the 1,500-man Brigade 2506 at Playa Girón. The first shots were fired not by the mercenaries but appropriately enough by the Texas-born CIA operative who accompanied them. Meanwhile Manuel Artime, the Cuban counterrevolutionary puppet chosen by the CIA to represent their hoped-for "government in arms," had picked up a handful of soil at the landing site and begun making a speech! The invasion force, too, anticipated being greeted as patriots by a good number of Cubans. As it turned out, only six local residents joined up with the brigade—among them the local bar owner and his son, as well as some foremen at a construction site.

Kennedy was counting on the brigade to hold the beachhead long enough to breed hoped-for resistance in Cuba and buy the U.S. government some time. Washington itself was not yet prepared militarily for an invasion. In October 1962, when the Pentagon *was* ready, it had begun assembling a 90,000-strong force. The mobilization then was so extensive that journalists began asking about the convoys and troop concentrations across the South, which couldn't be kept entirely under wraps. But in April 1961 Washington had only some 2,000 combat-ready U.S. marines on ships off Cuba—far from enough to carry out an invasion.

The U.S. rulers displayed a class blindness to the revolutionary capacities of ordinary workers and farmers in Cuba (and still do). But small groups of young people in a number of U.S. cities and on college campuses didn't. From the moment we learned of the invasion, we confidently asserted that, CIA-planted press dispatches to the contrary, the U.S.-organized mercenaries would be defeated. And we were reinforced in that conviction by the experienced communist workers, members of the Socialist Workers Party we had begun working alongside and had come to know and trust.

This confidence in the victory of the Cuban toilers was not just a matter of youthful enthusiasm for a revolution we deeply identified with. It was based in *fact*. And even if we couldn't explain it all at the time, we *acted* on the recognition that the Kennedy administration was operating on the basis of ideology, *not* fact.

Understanding this reality of class politics is something that comes only through struggle, and then studying, absorbing and generalizing the lessons of many struggles that came before. As working people begin to recognize the degree to which we ourselves are victims of bourgeois ideology, we also take strides toward greater class consciousness.

Recognizing how the class enemy operates also underlines why it's important for workers to be cautious about making fun of them. It's OK to do so sometimes, of course. In Fidel Castro's speech to the 1961 May Day demonstration in Havana printed in the new book, he points to the "wit and humor shown by several contingents of workers in the parade imitating the rich, with their elegant costumes and all the things typical of well-heeled youth from wealthy families." Comrades on a reporting trip to Cuba last month brought back some wonderful, forty-year-old photographs of these contingents!

But we should never poke fun in ways that may lead workers to underestimate the seriousness and ruthlessness of the class enemy. I was glad that a few days before press time on *Playa Girón* Pathfinder reversed its earlier decision to include in the photo insert a snapshot of Richard Bissell—the CIA official in charge of the Bay of Pigs operation—with one hand on the helm of his sailboat and a drink in the other.

It's not that the photo misrepresented Bissell. Like many in top CIA echelons, he was from a wealthy family and had been educated at exclusive private schools and Ivy League colleges such as Groton and Yale. Like John F. Kennedy and Robert F. Kennedy—both from a much wealthier, ruling-class family—Bissell was also a liberal Democrat, a sailor, and a cocktail man.

The original photo selection, however, could have been read as implying the false notion that the CIA's Bay of Pigs operation was an amateur-hour production, almost a clown show. *But it wasn't.* Fernández and Guevara are right: given the forces at the CIA's disposal, the invasion was well conceived and well executed from the standpoint of military strategy and tactics. What's more, career functionaries for the ruling class such as Bissell weren't lightweights. They put in many months and long hours—"unpaid," if you will; like professional revolutionaries, they have no concept of overtime pay—preparing the plan. The assault Bissell engineered was a murderous operation in which some 180 Cubans were killed, 300 were wounded or maimed, and substantial physical damage was inflicted. That's what's important to workers about how Bissell spent his time in 1960–61—not his hours at the helm of a sailboat.

That's one of the misconceptions about the Bay of Pigs we want to help counter with the new book. The battle wasn't primarily *bungled* by the CIA; it was *won* by the workers and farmers of revolutionary Cuba. What led to the outcome wasn't the military inadequacy of the imperialist rulers, something they could conceivably improve; it was their class political blindness, something they cannot change. And this blindness extended all the way from the White House, to the CIA, to the opinion molders, to the leadership of the mercenary brigade itself.

The most common rationalization in bourgeois circles for the

U.S. defeat at the Bay of Pigs is that Kennedy vacillated on the eve of the invasion by canceling a second round of air strikes on the morning of April 17. At the time, Bissell had been among the most fervent advocates of these "D-Day" strikes, which were supposed to take out Cuba's remaining combat planes. But in his memoirs, published shortly after his death in the mid-1990s, Bissell dismisses critics who "blame the whole thing on the president's last-minute decision to cancel the air strike." That decision alone "would not have ensured success," he says. "No one could say it would have."

Yes, "no one could." Especially since even the initial air strikes—when the U.S.-instigated forces held the element of surprise—succeeded in destroying only two of Cuba's twelve combat planes. By the time the April 17 raids were to have been attempted, the Revolutionary Air Force was already on maximum combat alert, its planes had been further dispersed, and antiaircraft batteries and other defensive measures had been reinforced around all Cuban airfields.

Fidel Castro made the right strategic decision on the first morning of the invasion to order the air force to focus on sinking the mercenaries' ammunition and supply ships, a mission the pilots carried out with stunning success. It's a myth, however, that by the final day of the battle the *gusanos* had nothing left to fight with but their fingers and fists. They certainly had more weapons and ammo than the Rebel Army ever had during the revolutionary war against Batista!

"What was our ammunition reserve?" during those years, Fidel asked in his April 23 report on the victory at Playa Girón. "The peasants used to go along the country roads picking up the stuff dropped by the enemy forces, and then brought the ammunition to us to fight with."

By comparison, Fidel said, all the Cuban people had to do was go down to Havana's Civic Plaza to look at the captured "antitank guns, mortars of all kinds, bazookas, automatic weapons, ammunition, communications equipment, all in enormous quantities."

As the foreword to *Playa Girón* concludes, "The invading forces lost the will to fight before they ran out of bullets. During three days of battle, they could never even get off the beaches, and additional U.S. air or naval support would have made no difference to the ultimate outcome." The great bulk of the brigade's cadres and officers had scattered into the woods three hours or more before the final surrender late in the afternoon.

It was the class character of the forces and their cause that made the difference at Playa Girón, not air strikes or ammunition. Some of the mercenaries may have convinced themselves they had enlisted in a noble crusade, and many used high-sounding words to drape their goal of taking back "their" factories, plantations, casinos, exclusive schools, country clubs, beaches, and servants. But in the last analysis, as Che pointed out, modern armies don't fight selflessly and to the death over the restoration of capitalist property.

The cadres of the people's militias, the Revolutionary National Police, the Rebel Army, and the Revolutionary Air Force, on the other hand, were fighting for something worth giving everything for at Playa Girón—something that was transforming the *life* of the great majority. They were fighting to defend what they had accomplished through two and a half years of a revolution, and the ways they were changing themselves in the process. They were fighting to defend the redemption of Cuba's national sovereignty and dignity from U.S. imperialism and its exploiting factory owners, landlords, and brothel and casino operators. To defend the land reform; the literacy campaign and universal public education; the enforcement of laws against racist discrimination; the slashing of housing rents and utility rates; the steps to draw workers, peasants, youth, and women more deeply into all aspects of economic, social, political, and military life; the internationalist solidarity with struggles by toilers throughout Latin America and the world.

That is the kind of army that can withstand big sacrifices and fight to the death. That is the kind of army that doesn't develop

"The invading forces lost their will to fight before they ran out of bullets."

Top: Revolutionary combatants at Playa Girón. Fidel Castro is in center hatch of tank. **Bottom:** Captured mercenaries after the battle. Almost 1,200 of the 1,500 invaders surrendered.

self-destructive doubts about what it is fighting for. That is the kind of army the enemy slowly but surely comes to realize won't stop doing battle, no matter what.

That's what's so telling about Fidel's story, in the 1961 May Day speech, about meeting with captured mercenaries a few days after the battle and asking if any of them had ever worked cutting sugarcane. Only one raised his hand.

Under certain circumstances, of course, overwhelming force with an unjust cause can overrun a small force with a just cause. The point is not to dismiss material realities. But not under conditions of a strengthening and consolidating socialist revolution, based among a toiling population that is armed and ready. *That's* why the invaders lost the will to fight. It was beaten out of them.

■

Politically understanding this helps us recognize where revolutionary discipline comes from, too. Effective discipline can never be imposed primarily from the outside. Many young workers start out being a bit uncomfortable with the word *discipline*, it seems to me, since in capitalist society it's so often associated with parental authority, teachers and truancy officers, preachers and priests, foremen and supervisors, or cops, courts, and parole officers. It's something inflicted on us, aimed at breaking our spirit and making us submissive to the norms and values demanded by capital.

But revolutionary discipline, proletarian discipline, is something that comes from within—something thinking and self-acting working people initiate and voluntarily submit to in order to advance common ends. It is a freely given response flowing from our political understanding that a centralized structure is essential to accomplish social goals that transcend the moment and that transcend the life of any individual.

José Ramón Fernández presents a compelling example in his testimony. He describes the situation late in the afternoon on the final day of the battle, April 19, when the victory was practically won. Less than two hours before taking Playa Girón, Fernández's forces spotted U.S. destroyers well within Cuba's territorial waters heading toward shore. Fernández ordered the troops to halt their advance along the beach and train their tank cannon and other heavy weapons toward the sea.

His only way of informing Fidel was to send a runner to the Australia Sugar Mill—they had no telephone or radio communications, no walkie-talkies. But there was a business phone still working at that mill from which a message could be relayed to the commander in chief who was elsewhere at the front. "Send me a battalion of infantry and a battalion of tanks because another landing is under way," Fernández says he wrote.

In the meantime, Fernández was on his own in deciding how to respond; there was no one of higher rank to turn to for orders. As the destroyers lowered landing craft and rowboats into the water, he ordered the troops to fire on the small craft with everything they had. "We did not fire on the U.S. destroyers, however," Fernández says, "although that's what many of our combatants wanted to do, inflamed by the battle and thinking about all the losses we had suffered. . . .

"You can imagine how difficult it was to forbid our troops to fire on the real invaders. While that decision might look to my subordinates like an act of weakness, however, I knew it was what had to be done. It was what the Revolution needed." Firing on the destroyers would have provided Washington with the pretext it had been looking for to rationalize an open assault, causing "irreparable harm to the Revolution and the country."

The U.S. destroyers soon headed back out to the high seas, recognizing the battle was lost and an evacuation attempt impossible, leaving their blood brothers high and dry. Fernández's forces took Playa Girón shortly afterwards. An hour and a half after he had sent off the runner to the sugar mill, "after all the fighting was over, Fidel's response came. 'They're just trying to escape from you. Grab them!'" That's what the forces under

Fernández's command had done. And the destroyers failed to rescue a single one of the invaders.

Looking back on the experience, Fernández acknowledges some embarrassment at not having recognized that the mercenaries and their U.S. sponsors were in no position to launch a second landing after the battering they had taken for three days. "I overestimated the enemy's combat will," he says.

But the discipline demonstrated in that situation—not just by Fernández, but by the young soldiers who carried out his order without necessarily thinking it was right—was decisive in securing the victory. It is a model for other revolutionaries.

It's a mistake for any one of us to imagine we'll never face a situation like this here in the U.S. class struggle. In fact, more than any other single thing, Fernández's story brought to mind a similar one in *Teamster Rebellion* told by Farrell Dobbs, a central leader of the 1934 Teamsters strikes in Minneapolis. Dobbs became one of the outstanding communist leaders in the United States and was national secretary of the SWP for almost twenty years.

The "hardest thing I ever did in my life," Farrell wrote, was to pitch in with other leaders of Teamsters Local 574 to confiscate weapons from his closest comrades-in-arms going out on picket duty in July 1934, just days after the cops had opened fire on unarmed workers. Two workers had been murdered, and nearly seventy strikers and bystanders wounded.

"This was a situation in which the central strike leadership"— Farrell, still in his late twenties, was among the youngest—"had to act swiftly and decisively. Otherwise impulsive pickets, looking for a showdown with the cops, could have done irreparable damage to the union's cause. . . . Understandably, we got some stiff arguments and some uncomplimentary descriptions of our attitude.

"In the end, however," Farrell said, "the weapons were handed over, thanks to the union's well-established disciplinary norms and to the leadership authority we had earned" in previous battles.

Discipline is not a military quality first and foremost. Nor is it primarily an organizational or administrative question. It is among the deepest questions of *working-class politics*. It is the recognition by growing numbers of workers and farmers that we need centralized structures—class-struggle unions, a revolutionary army, and above all a proletarian communist party—in order to join together, fight effectively, organize retreats and advances, and win.

Workers and farmers don't have the wealth, the educational or media institutions, or the military might of big capital. But revolutionary centralism—if we'll work together to forge it and become habituated to it—allows the working class and our exploited allies to leverage and deploy the weapons we *do* have: solidarity and imagination.

■

One sentence in the foreword to *Playa Girón*, more than any other, captures politically what I hope each of us takes away from this meeting today. It's from a March 13, 1961, speech by Fidel Castro, given as Washington was accelerating its campaign of terror aimed at overturning the Cuban Revolution. The talk marked the fourth anniversary of the armed assault organized by the Revolutionary Directorate on the Presidential Palace of the U.S.-backed dictator Fulgencio Batista in which student leader José Antonio Echeverría was killed.

There is one thing the Cuban people "can tell Mr. Kennedy," Castro said to the cheering crowd. "A victorious revolution will be seen in the United States before a victorious counterrevolution in Cuba."

We're convinced that sentence remains as accurate today as it was in 1961. It's not a prediction; it's not an encouraging clap on the back. It's the recognition of how capitalism works, of the line of march of working people, and of the communist caliber of the revolutionary movement in Cuba. For revolutionists in the United States, in Cuba, and around the world, it sharply poses Lenin's famous question: What is to be done?

Fidel's assertion makes quite a statement about the Cuban Revolution—even more so forty years later, if you think about it, than it did at the time. And it was quite a statement in 1961! Today we know that the revolution in the United States will take place *after* Fidel and the generation that organized and led the Cuban Revolution are no longer part of the leadership in Cuba. So when we say the statement remains true today, we're saying something about the continuity of revolutionary leadership not only in Cuba but its interconnection with the continuity and renewal of communist leadership in the United States and around the world.

In Richard Bissell's memoirs, he reports that during top-level White House discussions of the invasion plans in 1961, Secretary of State Dean Rusk, drawing on much experience, used to ask "whether something couldn't be done with 'silver bullets'"—in plainer words, wasn't it possible to buy off a substantial number of Cuban leaders? "His impression was that even in a well-run covert operation one should try to bribe one's enemies rather than fight them."

Bissell then comments, with no explanation, that "unfortunately, this would not have worked in Cuba."

He was correct, but why wouldn't it have worked? The reason has everything to do with Yankee imperialism's misestimation of the workers and peasants of Cuba. The U.S. rulers were functioning on the basis of false analogies at every level. They were acting based on the distortions viewed through the lens of their class. That fact helps us understand why the course of the Cuban Revolution and prospects for the coming American revolution have been hitched together so closely for more than four decades. It underlines the indispensable continuity of the revolutionary workers movement going back to the October 1917 Bolshevik Revolution in Russia and, even further back, to the founding of modern communism and the work of an internationalist communist party in the time of Karl Marx and Frederick Engels 150 years ago.

Above all, if the "silver bullets" could have worked in Cuba, then we'd have to conclude that Fidel's March 1961 declaration to Mr. Kennedy was not a statement of fact but an article of faith, not a course of revolutionary action but an exhortation, just bravado. Just bidding up the price.

■

The foreword to the new book, *Playa Girón*, is based largely on the story of the activity a number of young people—I was one of them—carried out on a campus in Minnesota in the months leading up to, during, and after the Bay of Pigs invasion. Those experiences were important to record, we thought, since they are a concrete example of how the advance of the Cuban Revolution has been intertwined with the class struggle in the United States and building the communist movement here.

Revolutionists in Cuba become very interested when they learn how great moments in their history have had a political impact on youth and working people in this country. And aside from finding out about such moments from other revolutionists, they have very few ways of doing so. That's one of the things Mary-Alice Waters, Martín Koppel, and I discovered in October 1997 when we conducted three of the interviews that appear in Pathfinder's book, *Making History*.

The interviews had been set up sometime earlier so we could meet with three generals of Cuba's Revolutionary Armed Forces who had been leaders of the combat forces that defeated the invaders at Playa Girón. These included José Ramón Fernández. (For that reason, by the way, *Making History* is must reading for anyone who enjoys the book we're celebrating here today.) As it happened, however, we ended up conducting the interviews during the month marking the thirty-fifth anniversary of the October "Missile" Crisis. And we found that the generals took great interest in the protests and other efforts to get out the truth that had been organized by communists and other supporters of the Cuban Revolution in the United States during those dangerous days in 1962. Just as they were interested to learn of the work we had organized a year and a half earlier in response to the Bay of Pigs invasion.

We should recall that only a matter of days after their defeat at Playa Girón, the Kennedy administration began making plans for an invasion force of tens of thousands of soldiers to assault Cuba. The invasion was to be the culmination of a stepped-up program of covert air and sea attacks, terrorist activity, economic sabotage—and assassinations. By the end of 1961 these plans had been formalized as Operation Mongoose, with Brigadier General Edward Lansdale formally in charge. But this time around the operation was organized directly out of the White House under the supervision of the president and his brother Robert F. Kennedy, who was attorney general.

"Robert Kennedy's involvement in organizing and directing Mongoose became so intense," Bissell says in his memoirs, "that he might as well have been deputy director for plans for the operations"—that was Bissell's own official title in the CIA, a euphemism for head of the agency's covert activities.

"Operation Mongoose was a more ambitious and more massive paramilitary activity than the Bay of Pigs had been," Bissell continues. "[I]t involved significantly more personnel, as well as hit-and-run raids. . . . Operation Mongoose was closely monitored by the chief of state, and all actions received his explicit authorization."

One of the recently declassified Mongoose "memorandums for the record" recounts a March 1962 meeting in the Oval Office to discuss a proposed plan to assassinate Fidel Castro during a visit to novelist Ernest Hemingway's former home near Havana. The memo, drafted by Lansdale, reported "agreement that the matter was *so delicate and sensitive* that it shouldn't be surfaced to the Special Group"—the joint CIA–Pentagon–White House body chaired by Robert Kennedy that oversaw Mongoose—"until we were ready to go, and then not in detail. I pointed out that this all pertained to *fractioning the regime*"—a code word for assassination.

"If it happened," the memo concluded, "it could develop like a brushfire, much as in Hungary, and we must be prepared to help it win our goal of Cuba freed of a Communist government."

It's the memo's reference to Hungary that I want to call to your attention. Lansdale was drawing an analogy to the Hungarian Revolution of October 1956. Armed workers had risen up against the brutal Stalinist regime and established revolutionary councils in Hungary that year, before being crushed by Soviet tanks a few weeks later.

But this Operation Mongoose memorandum is another example of the U.S. rulers being taken in by their own ideology. Because the socialist revolution in Cuba is not some variant of a Stalinist regime—one with broader popular support to begin with, perhaps, but nonetheless fundamentally alien to the toilers. To the contrary, the revolutionary government in Cuba—a workers and peasants regime, the dictatorship of the proletariat—is the *opposite* of the regimes of a privileged, petty-bourgeois caste in Hungary, the Soviet Union, China, Vietnam, or anywhere else. Just as Stalinism itself is not a degenerate form of Bolshevism but its negation—a counterrevolutionary current that emerged and crystallized in deadly opposition to the continuity of Lenin's course and its proletarian internationalist foundations.

As proven at Playa Girón, and then once again a year and a half later in October 1962, the workers and peasants of Cuba weren't biding their time, waiting for some external shock in order to rise up and overthrow the revolutionary government. Instead, on both occasions they mobilized in the millions to defend their national sovereignty and their socialist revolution.

Fidel Castro has referred to the collapse of the regimes in the Soviet Union and Eastern Europe as "the fall of the meringue." There was no meringue in Cuba, at the opening of the 1960s or today.

■

The foreword to *Playa Girón* also shows how natural mass work is to militants who have not been pushed, as a result of a prolonged working-class retreat, into what Farrell Dobbs once described as a semisectarian existence.

The young people at Carleton College whose story during the battle at Girón is told in the foreword had received no systematic political training prior to our activity in 1960–61 in defense of the Cuban Revolution. Some of us had been involved in civil rights actions beforehand, such as picketing Woolworth's stores to support desegregation efforts in the South. In my own case, I had also paid my dollar to join the Young Socialist Alliance in the middle of my senior year, but I was the only YSA member on campus and my membership remained largely nominal until after I graduated.

As the foreword explains, we were fortunate that some veteran worker-bolsheviks in Minneapolis-St. Paul took a real interest in us. A number of them had substantial experience in labor battles, including V.R. Dunne, who had been a cadre of the communist movement in the United States from its founding in 1919 and a leader of the Teamster battles in the 1930s. Like us, they were determined partisans of the Cuban Revolution and its leadership, and they were joining in protest meetings and rallies and using the *Militant* to help get out the truth to co-workers and others. That political collaboration opened whole new vistas to us.

Despite our inexperience, however, the activity we carried out at Carleton, described in the foreword, was a model of mass work in many ways. We had probably never heard that term at the time, but that's what we were doing. And it's something the cadres in the workers-district branches and union fractions of the Socialist Workers Party, as well as the Young Socialists, can learn from still today.

Several leaders of this activity at Carleton were already on our way to becoming revolutionaries at the time. We took that for granted. But the most important point is that we worked hard at collaborating with those who weren't yet revolutionaries—or who were never going to become revolutionaries—but who for their own reasons opposed U.S. military aggression against a sovereign nation. Or who were outraged that the administration and faculty wouldn't grant recognition to a campus chapter of the Fair Play for Cuba Committee. Or who were disgusted that some well-known liberal professors wouldn't even show up at the faculty meeting where recognition was on the agenda, much less raise their hands in favor, because they feared their jobs were on the line.

What's more, we were always straight with everyone we worked with. We said who we were, and we never maneuvered anybody. We acted on the understanding—even if we hadn't yet internalized all its political implications—that the habits of loyalty and trustworthiness are the bedrock of any effective mass work. Doing so, in turn, helped prepare us to understand more deeply later on why such habits are not just a precondition of elementary class solidarity and trade unionism, but of the revolutionary centralism at the heart of the most advanced formation of the working class, a communist party.

We never harbored the illusion we could strengthen our ranks, or win over those not yet convinced, by trying somehow to shut up or suppress the views of those who supported the U.S. government's course or who were open right-wingers. We took them on politically, exposed their lies, and rebutted their arguments. That's what the war of the bulletin boards described in the foreword was all about. That's why we launched the Challenge speakers program—to broaden the spectrum of views available, including very controversial views, and increase the openness to debate. It was a way to bring some political life to the campus. It helped tie together those engaged in activities in support of Black rights, against the witch-hunting House Un-American Activities Committee, in opposition to the nuclear weapons policies of the imperialist regimes, against U.S. military intervention in Laos, and in support of the Cuban Revolution.

Students who didn't initially believe what we were saying about the U.S.-organized terrorist campaign against the people of Cuba would see a photograph or read an article about the torture and murder of a literacy volunteer, then come hear a speaker, have some informal discussion afterwards, and over time change their minds. The big shift, as the foreword explains, came with the victory by the Cuban toilers at Playa Girón. Beforehand fewer than a half dozen of us had been active in Cuba solidarity work at Carleton, but after the victory our ranks expanded rapidly, virtually exploded.

We had to learn the realities everyone bumps up against when you get involved in mass work. All of a sudden, as the foreword describes, the polite college discourse gave way to McCarthyite-style red-baiting and threats by the decorous dean of the college. A few weeks later, on the day of the first triumphalist wire-service accounts of the invasion, chants of "War! War! War!" broke out in the largest dormitory dining room. As the stakes increased, so did the sorting process. Some who hadn't been with us earlier went through a profound political transformation during those weeks in 1961 and set off down a lifetime course that brought them into the communist movement. Others who had been with us before the heat was turned up saw comfortable futures in the academic community flash before their eyes, and made an about-face.

And we discovered that while we had to answer the arguments of both liberals and conservatives, under slightly sharpened conditions we also had to be ready to do something else. We had to be ready to fight right-wing thugs in order to defend our right to organize a meeting or hold a public protest. The assault by the reactionary Young Americans for Freedom and others on a Bay of Pigs speak-out at the University of Minnesota (as well as protests in several other cities and towns) is also described in the foreword.

Only a year and a half later, in October 1962, twenty-two students at the University of Indiana in Bloomington protesting the U.S. government's naval blockade and invasion threats against Cuba were physically attacked by thugs among a hostile crowd of thousands of flag-waving students and townspeople. Three YSA members who had helped organize that Cuba solidarity action were subsequently indicted in May 1963 under the state Anti-Communism Act for advocating the over-throw of the U.S. government and the State of Indiana, charges with a sentence of one to three years imprisonment if upheld.

The pretext for the indictments was the participation by the three students in a campus meeting at which a YSA leader who was Black, on a national speaking tour, described the current stage of the Black rights movement and spoke in support of the right of self-defense against racist terror. The YSA published the full text of his talk as a pamphlet. It took a nearly four-year-long international defense campaign before we forced Monroe County to drop the witch-hunting indictments against the Bloomington students.

Throughout all these experiences, the veteran communists we had gotten to know in Minneapolis-St. Paul helped us keep our eyes focused on what needed to be done in the United States to build a revolutionary movement *here*. Several of us at Carleton had spent some time in Cuba in 1960, and a couple of us had been there long enough to become friends with some young militia members and other revolutionaries. During the days of the Bay of Pigs invasion, when I said something slightly self-pitying over the phone to Ray Dunne about feeling guilty about not being there with them in Cuba, Ray was comradely but unsympathetic: "You have no doubts about what the people you became closest with in Cuba are doing," he told me. "They're fighting. And they assume you're doing the same thing, wherever you are. So you better prove them right and stop pandering to your emotions."

That was a good lesson—and a memorable one. If that hadn't become our attitude, then we would have never truly become revolutionary internationalists in practice. And the statement by Fidel I read earlier would have no meaning for us.

The communist movement in the United States attracted revolutionary-minded young people to its ranks under the transforming impact of the Cuban Revolution. At Carleton alone over the next few years, many students were won to the Young Socialist Alliance in the course of the activities we've described here or by those directly involved in them. A big majority, close to a dozen, either remain active in our movement to this day, almost forty years later, or did so for the rest of their lives.

■

We're at a turning point of a certain kind in working-class politics in the United States.

Communist workers recognized several years ago that a decade-long retreat of our class was bottoming out and that we had entered a period of renewed resistance by workers and farmers. It's not primarily that for the first time in quite a while we are seeing a few more victories in strikes and organizing drives, which we are. But even in the still-more-typical struggles that end in standoffs with the bosses, we are finding groups of workers who remain ready for a fight, who are reaching out to extend support to other struggles, who are open to new and radical ideas about the root causes of the economic and social ills facing working people and to broadening views of solidarity.

The pace of the manifestations of this sea change in the class struggle, of course, goes through ebbs and flows. Resistance speeds up and broadens for a while, and then slows down. The unions, the sole mass institutions of the American labor movement today, continue to weaken. The traditions promoted by the union officialdom—a product of their bourgeois outlook and values, and their petty-bourgeois conditions of life—leave them utterly unready for what can suddenly erupt under the current crises-ridden conditions of world capitalism. Above all they are unprepared for the struggles building up underneath, not to mention frightened by that prospect. They, too, can never understand the capacities of the ranks.

For most of the past decade, we heard more and more from the big-business press and capitalist politicians about the "new economy." The new era capitalism had entered, we were told, was fueled by a computer-driven "productivity miracle." Growing numbers of bourgeois spokespeople went so far as to suggest that recessions and business cycles were a thing of the past.

Today, however, a few more facts are coming out that confirm what communist workers have been explaining all along.

First, to the degree there's been an increase over the past decade in what the bourgeoisie measures as labor productivity—and it's far from the ballyhooed "miracle"—the source has not been computers and the Internet. The bosses have boosted their profit margins by cutting real wages and benefits, speeding up production, lengthening the workweek, increasing part-time and temporary labor, and reducing government-funded social security programs. And because of the misleadership of the labor movement, the employing class has largely been able to get away with it.

Second, the long upturn in the business cycle during the 1990s—and it was long by capitalist standards, going on ten years—was not based on a historic acceleration of capacity-expanding capital investment. It was not based on drawing more and more workers into plants, mines, and mills and massively increasing the production of salable goods. It was not based, in short, on a major expansion of social wealth. Instead, the long upturn was the product of a giant speculative bubble, an enormous mountain of debt.

While stock prices as measured by the Dow Jones Industrial Average, for example, rose 225 percent between 1994 and the Dow's high point in January 2000 (and that's staid compared to the more than 500 percent increase in the high-tech-heavy NASDAQ stock index over that same period), the Gross Domestic Product of the United States rose only a little more than 25 percent and corporate profits around 65 percent. In fact, while the total market value of all stocks issued in the United States as measured by their share prices had never risen much above 75 percent of GDP in the twentieth century (and then only on the eve of the 1929 crash that ushered in the Great Depression), it shot up to 175 percent of GDP in the late 1990s.

As for debt levels, corporate indebtedness exploded in the latter half of the 1990s. It was fueled in part by a spate of multibillion-dollar mergers that substantially increased the concentration of capital in the United States even further. Debt levels surpassed those reached even during the borrowing binge of the 1980s, which in turn had helped set the stage for the 1987 stock market crash. Last year alone corporate debt shot up by nearly half a trillion dollars.

And personal debt has rocketed to record levels, as most of us know concretely from our co-workers, family members, friends, and credit card bills.

Layoffs, too, have begun to climb sharply since the end of last year. So too the number of workers filing claims for unemployment benefits. The flip side of the employers' drive to maintain low, "just-in-time inventories" has been an increase in the volatility of the demand for labor—including an explosive growth of temporary jobs, or what some big-business writers and economists callously label "just-in-time labor."

So, the vulnerability of world capitalism to sudden and destabilizing shocks is being confirmed, despite the bourgeois triumphalism of much of the 1990s. A further deepening of the farm crisis, a spread of the California power breakdown, the bankruptcy of another debt-wracked Wall Street "hedge fund" that holds the big banks in bondage, a financial collapse beginning in Argentina or Indonesia, a plunge in the dollar's value, a rash of bank failures stemming from these or other jolts—these are just a few of the myriad possible developments that can plunge workers and farmers in the United States and other imperialist countries into a deepening social and economic crisis.

Throughout Africa and much of Latin America and Asia, of course, hundreds of millions are already facing a downward-spiraling catastrophe, and have been for almost two decades. Even in the most devastated areas of the semicolonial world, a tiny handful of privileged families have prospered, however, as well as a larger middle class and pockets of toilers in various countries. What's more, the effects of the capitalist crisis have been very uneven and polarized, giving rise to the illusion in certain parts of Latin America and particularly Asia (the "Ti-

gers") that applications remain open to join the club of indus-
trially advanced capitalist nations. But the workings of the
market system, and the class structure it unrelentingly repro-
duces and reinforces worldwide, are once again confirming what
Lenin explained to workers and farmers on the eve of the Russian Revolution in his booklet *Imperialism: The Highest Stage of
Capitalism*—that by the opening of the twentieth century the
doors to that exclusive club had been slammed shut once and
for all.

The current officialdom of the labor movement in the United
States seek to avert their eyes from these realities. To prepare
for battle means you might end up having to fight one, and
that's exactly the unsettling prospect union bureaucrats fear
most. They have no intention of doing so.

But the explosive mixture building up in the United States is
being enriched by the ongoing shift in the composition of the
working class in this country. Immigration is changing the face
of the working population in virtually every imperialist country except Japan. But nowhere to the same degree as right here.
Nowhere.

In search of inexpensive labor, U.S. finance capital continues
to draw in toilers driven off the land and left without jobs or
livelihoods throughout the Third World. It draws in workers
who are determined to take advantage of its relatively higher
wages to support families and get a grubstake. Over the past
half decade, the United States has taken in roughly half of all
emigrants to the imperialist countries—one half! The U.S. rulers know that these massive labor inflows are essential to the
"productivity miracle" and profit drive that are central to further widening their edge over capitalist rivals in Germany,
France, Japan, and elsewhere in Europe and Asia.

As a result of this immigration, New York City has grown by
nearly 10 percent in as many years, and Chicago and several
other cities that had declined in population over the half century since World War II increased in size during the 1990s.
Nearly 11 percent of the U.S. population today is foreign-born,

and the percentage of immigrants in the ranks of the working class is substantially higher than that.

At the opening of the twenty-first century, the United States is the only country in the imperialist world whose rate of population growth is increasing not declining; it is also the imperialist country in which the median age is rising most slowly.

The American working class is getting *younger*. And the implications of that fact for prospects to transform the labor movement and build a revolutionary proletarian party are a pleasure to behold.

What it means to be an "American worker" today is changing. The experience and traditions—and image—of the working class and labor movement in the United States are being enriched by the diverse cultures and lessons of struggles by workers and peasants from Latin America and the Caribbean, from Asia and the Pacific, from Africa, the Middle East, and elsewhere. In the course of common struggles, and through growing recognition that solidarity is essential, these workers are finding ways to communicate with each other. They are finding ways to work, and more and more often to fight, shoulder to shoulder.

Most important, the communist movement in the United States—through the mix of workplaces and unions where we find jobs; through the workers districts where we locate our halls and bookstores; through our regular Militant Labor Forums; through our efforts to produce and sell periodicals, books, and pamphlets in both English and Spanish, and as much as possible in French—is beginning to find more and more ways for the activity, composition, and leadership of the revolutionary party to reflect this changing American working class.

Some of you may recall that in the late 1980s supporters of Pathfinder Press organized artists from around the world to paint a six-story mural on the side of its building. The large banner across the bottom of that mural declared, in English, Spanish, and French: "For a world without borders. Por un mundo sin fronteras. Pour un monde sans frontières." Among other things, that slogan was connected to a number of struggles we were involved in at the time to prevent the U.S. government from deporting several fighters back into the hands of cops and jailers in Mexico, Northern Ireland, and elsewhere. And we always pointed out that while a world without borders is impossible to achieve under capitalism, *the fight for that goal* is an essential part of mobilizing the class forces to overturn that brutal and oppressive social system in country after country worldwide.

This transformation of the working class in the United States and other imperialist countries is *irreversible*. The capitalists can pull 'em in, but they can't push 'em out.

Toilers impressed into debt slavery by domestic exploiters and imperialism in their countries of birth are pouring into this country and becoming wage slaves. For the U.S. ruling families, that process is a more and more indispensable engine of capital accumulation. As they inflate more and bigger balloons of debt worldwide in hopes of counteracting capitalist overproduction and clearing world markets, those who are the hardest-hit victims of indebtedness are joining other gravediggers of the imperialist global order right here in its strongest bastion.

Class-conscious workers glory in these historic changes. We glory in these reinforcement brigades coming to the aid of our class, refreshing the heterogeneity and richness of the labor movement. The historic wave of immigration transforms the proletarian movement in the United States into something more and more recognizable as the class that will overthrow capitalism.

■

The battles we and other workers are and will be engaged in are being prepared on many fronts by the course of the ruling class.

Workers who have studied and absorbed some of the hard-earned lessons of our class—who have started to use the political arsenal published and distributed by Pathfinder, the cumu-

lative record of more than 150 years of struggle the world over—
can help other working people better understand the source of
our exploitation and oppression. We can help fellow workers
and farmers recognize that the conditions we face are a product
of how capitalism *works*, not how it sometimes doesn't work.
We can help them see that the root of our problems is not one or
the other of the bosses' parties—the Republicans but not the
Democrats, or vice versa. Nor is it the union misleaders, whose
class-collaborationist course does hamper our capacity to fight
effectively and win.

Our class enemy is the capitalists themselves and the two-
party system that in the United States serves as the central political prop of their rule. We have no common interests with the
capitalists. Everything they try to tell us about "our country,"
"our way of life," "our language," "our industry," "our factory"
are lies. The "our" is the heart of the lie. It's a diversion aimed
at dividing us from those with whom we *do* have common
interests—the workers, farmers, and exploited toilers of all countries. All of us share the same class enemies: the imperialist ruling classes, and the domestic landlords and capitalists dominated by imperialism the world over. That's the only "we" and
"they" that has any meaning for working people.

William Clinton, the politician whom liberals, with a straight
face, sometimes described as the first Black president, has recently left office. From the beginning eight years ago, communist workers insisted that Clinton was no friend of the working
class, that he would be a war president, a prison president, a
death-penalty president—in short, a president, like those before him, whose course at home and abroad was aimed at serving the class interests of the U.S. ruling families. The same is
true of Clinton's successor, George W. Bush, and of the bipartisan Congress, then and now.

Just hours before Bush was sworn in last January 20, Clinton
ordered U.S. warplanes to bomb civilian targets in southern Iraq.
Then, less than a month later, Bush sent U.S. planes to hit neighborhoods on the outskirts of Baghdad, dropping twenty-eight

cluster bombs. These weapons, which scatter thousands of small explosive devices, are designed with one and only one purpose in mind: to kill and maim, to mangle the flesh of the maximum number of men, women, and children. (The *Militant* was the only newspaper where you could have found out about the cluster bombs, unless you happened to catch the *Washington Post* on-line on February 26. The *Post* editors made sure the article never made it into the print edition.)

The assaults on Iraq by Clinton and Bush were a virtual replay of the handoff eight years earlier from the elder Bush to Clinton. During the days prior to the January 1993 inauguration, the outgoing Republican administration rained down bombs on Iraq, and the new administration followed suit the very next week. Ever since then, the U.S. and British armed forces have kept up the bombing of Iraq virtually nonstop; the United Nations reported that on average one Iraqi civilian was killed in such raids every other day in 1999 and 2000. Others have been wounded, many mutilated for life.

Washington's use of the heinous cluster bombs against the Iraqi people should remind us of something else in Fernández's testimony. The Cuban general reports there that the U.S. government supplied the mercenaries at the Bay of Pigs with napalm bombs, which they used against Cuba's defending forces. Citing a published account by one of the mercenary pilots, Fernández says the invaders' planes carried three tons of these weapons, which spray an incendiary jelly that clings to the flesh of human beings, burning and asphyxiating them to death. International rules of war signed by governments the world over, Fernández told the Havana court, forbid the use of "weapons, projectiles, and materials designed to cause that kind of harm contrary to the normal laws of humanity. But those were precisely the type of bombs used by the armed forces of the United States."

To the degree many of us are aware of the U.S. rulers' use of napalm, we often associate it exclusively with the monstrous suffering inflicted by Washington on tens of thousands of peasants and workers during the Vietnam War. But it had been used beforehand by U.S. imperialism against the Japanese in the Pacific, during Washington's barbaric razing to the ground of northern Korea a few years later, and against the Cuban people at the Bay of Pigs. (It was used by French imperialism during its unsuccessful wars to crush the Algerian and Vietnamese independence struggles, too.)

We can point to many other examples of these bipartisan war policies.

Even though Big Oil Bush won't be inclined to match the record of the most pro-Israeli president since Harry Truman, his administration nonetheless will continue the course of the Clinton White House in supporting Tel Aviv's murderous assaults on Palestinians fighting for the return of their homeland.

Both parties will press their efforts in the Balkans—from Bosnia and Serbia, to Kosova and now Macedonia—to overturn the conquests of the Yugoslav Revolution, restore capitalist relations there, and reinforce the weight of U.S. imperialism as the dominant "European" military power. The differences will be over how to do this most effectively.

Under Clinton the expansion of NATO has extended the reach of Washington's armed might right up to the borders of the former Soviet Union. During the presidential campaign both Albert Gore and George W. Bush advocated further expansion, with the next countries in line—Lithuania, Latvia, and Estonia—bringing imperialist military pressure even closer to the main urban centers of the workers state in Russia.

The Clinton and Bush administrations, with bipartisan backing in Congress, have pressed forward with plans for an antiballistic missile system. Washington aims to establish a U.S. nuclear first-strike capacity against all the other world powers with nuclear arsenals, from Moscow to Paris and London. As the U.S. rulers did with the founding of NATO in 1949, they intend *above all* to leverage military power to increase their political dominance vis-à-vis "Europe."

More immediately, a U.S. antiballistic missile system will be targeted against China and North Korea, two countries in Asia where the imperialist yoke was thrown off and capitalist social relations overturned half a century ago. Washington already has hundreds of nuclear-tipped missiles targeted on these two countries. In addition, the U.S. rulers seek to instill terror into the government of any semicolonial country—Iraq, Iran, India, Pakistan—that has built missile-based defenses that could be used against future imperialist aggression. The plans already begun under Clinton for an Alaska-based Theater Missile Defense system will serve as the starting point for more extensive Star Wars proposals by the Bush administration, whose heart will be a submarine-based and space-based attack platform to go after missiles in the boost phase.

Finally, with particular regard to the occasion of today's celebration, we must point to the overwhelming bipartisan support for Washington's ongoing, forty-year-long economic, political, and military aggression against the Cuban Revolution. During his final months in office, Clinton signed an agricultural appropriations bill that—in addition to lining the pockets of agribusiness and capitalist farmers at the expense of working farmers—contained a rider making long-standing administrative restrictions on travel to Cuba federal law. Now U.S. residents who visit Cuba face criminal, in addition to civil, penalties.

Among hostile acts over his eight years—acts too numerous to review—Clinton in 1996 signed into law the "Cuban Liberty and Democratic Solidarity (Libertad) Act," also known as the Helms-Burton Law, which tightened the U.S. economic embargo against Cuba. Four years earlier, as the Democratic candidate in 1992, he led the charge in championing another reinforcement of Washington's economic war against Cuba, the misnamed Cuban Democracy Act or Torricelli Act, which the still-serving Republican president then signed. The new Bush administration, in both word and deed, is now carrying out its own campaign pledge to continue along this course.

The war against working people at home by the employers and their two parties has deepened on many fronts, as well.

• A landmark of this assault, both for the Clinton administration and the Republican-controlled Congress, was the so-called Personal Responsibility and Work Opportunity Reconciliation Act of 1996. This legislation eliminated Aid to Families with Dependent Children and limited welfare payments to any particular family to a lifetime total of five years. Clinton's "reform" was more than an incarnation of his reactionary campaign pledge four years earlier "to end welfare as we know it." It was the biggest single success of the rulers so far in beginning to erode the federal Social Security system—a conquest won by working people through the struggles that built the industrial unions in the 1930s, and substantially extended through the mass civil rights movement of the 1960s.

Shortly before leaving office, Clinton boasted that 8 million people nationwide had been slashed from state welfare rolls—a 60 percent drop. What the bourgeois supporters of this legislation don't trumpet so loudly, however, is that the vast majority of these individuals, if they've been able to find work at all, have been pressed into jobs at minimum wage or close to it, with few if any health or pension benefits. And that's been during the high point of the upturn in the capitalist business cycle. As the first targets of the legislation's five-year limit are cut off permanently from welfare payments in the months ahead, they will find themselves in the midst of the layoffs and rising unemployment we've already described.

It's useful to remember that Clinton's welfare legislation—not just its basic provisions, but *name* and all—was taken over lock, stock, and barrel from a plank in the so-called Contract for America promised by the Newt Gingrich–led Republican majority that swept into Congress in 1994.

The 1996 act was the first time in nearly two-thirds of a century that an entire category of working people—single mothers and their children—have been eliminated from the kinds of protections Social Security has guaranteed for retirees, children, workers injured or thrown out of a job, and others vulnerable to the instabilities and devastations inherent in capitalism, both in good times and bad. What's more, this is a section of the working class that is expanding in the United States: nearly a third of all children today are born to women who begin raising them in so-called single-parent households, which currently make up roughly half of all family units.

Like the change in the composition of the working class with the growing weight of immigrant workers, this change in the family structure is also irreversible—a product of the greater economic independence women have achieved as a result of their increasing integration into the workforce, and of the social gains of struggles for women's liberation. The poverty and social crisis this also entails for millions of working-class women and children registers the reality of class relations under capitalism and the fact that only a socialist revolution can open the door to the transformation of these oppressive social relations.

• The new Bush administration, despite its election campaign rhetoric, is no more likely than its predecessors to attempt a head-on assault against the 1973 *Roe v. Wade* Supreme Court ruling decriminalizing abortion. At the same time, the very workings of the capitalist system will combine with the consequences of the rulers' assault on the living standards of working people to continue reducing access to abortion procedures. With no medical facilities today providing abortions in a third of all cities and nearly 90 percent of counties in the United States, the costs of travel and lodging alone mean that working-class women are at a disadvantage. Never mind the numerous other obstacles related to age and "consent" by parents, waiting periods, and mandatory counseling about "alternatives" that have been enacted by various state governments.

• With support from both parties in Congress, Clinton signed into law legislation that expanded mandatory prison sentences and increased their length, reduced protections against arbitrary search and seizure by the cops and courts, increased property seizures *before* trials, and financed a record increase of more murderously armed police on the streets.

• Both Clinton and Bush can lay justified claim to the shameful designation: the "death-penalty president." Clinton advocated and signed legislation significantly expanding the number of federal crimes punishable by death, and presided over a major reduction in the right of death-row prisoners to submit habeas corpus petitions for federal court review of their cases. For his part, while Bush was on the presidential campaign trail in 2000, the state of Texas, of which he was governor at the time, carried out the legal murder of the largest number of prisoners ever in any state in a single year in American history; what's more, those forty were only a quarter of the executions carried out during Bush's six years in the statehouse.

• During the eight years of the Clinton presidency, the number of people locked behind bars in U.S. prisons doubled to two million. While the United States has 5 percent of the world's population, today it has 25 percent of the world's prisoners. As throughout history, the overwhelming majority of those incarcerated are toilers, with the hammer falling most heavily on those who are Black, Latino, or Native American. Fully one of every three young Black males today is either in prison, on parole, or on probation. Lockdowns and solitary confinement, with all their dehumanizing effects on the human spirit, have increasingly become the norm.

• The number of privatized "services," even privately owned prisons, continues to increase, and now we are witnessing the relentless growth of a concomitant: prison labor. The *Wall Street Journal* a few days ago featured an article on the expansion of programs to hire out inmates in state-operated prisons. Pointing to the emergence of what it calls "the convict version of Kelly Girls," the article was headlined: "Prison as Profit Center: Inmates' Labor, Expenditures Enhance the Bottom Line; Temp Agency Behind Bars."

In Oregon prisons, the article explains, "employers offer no retirement, vacation, or health benefits; nor do they pay for Social Security, workers' compensation, or Medicare. . . . [H]iring inmates can cut an employer's payroll costs by 35%." As a re-

sult, it adds, "businessmen now all but beg for prison labor."
Just like the good old days—New Economy chain gangs.

Prisons certified by the federal Prison Industry Enhancement
program, the article continues, get a bonus; they are allowed to
sell the products of prison labor in interstate commerce. Prisoners covered by this U.S. government "incentive" program
must "be allowed to keep at least"—in other words, no more
than—"20% of what they earn. The rest of their wages can be
withheld to pay income taxes, child-support obligations, room-
and-board charges, and payments due to victim-assistance
funds."

• In 1996 Clinton signed into law the Illegal Immigration
Reform and Immigrant Responsibility Act, adopted by a Republican Congress. That law expands the powers of the Immigration and Naturalization Service (INS) to round up and de-
port those charged with being "illegal" immigrants without the
right to judicial review or appeal. Simultaneously the White
House and Congress funded the expansion of the hated *la migra*
into the largest federal cop agency, one that has stepped up factory raids and deportations to record numbers in recent years.

Far from aiming to stem the inflow of labor from the Americas and elsewhere, the rulers intend for their repressive measures to heighten insecurity and fear among immigrants, hop-
ing to maintain them as a superexploitable labor pool and
discourage involvement in unionization efforts and other social struggles and political fights.

• Under the Star Chamber provisions of the 1996 Anti-
Terrorism and Effective Death Penalty Act, the U.S. government
has held some two dozen people without bail in "preventive
detention" on the basis of "secret evidence." Most are immigrants from Arab or other majority Muslim countries accused
of links with "terrorist organizations"—the code word the U.S.
rulers increasingly use to rationalize both assaults on democratic rights at home and military strikes abroad. Altogether
some 20,000 people are being held in U.S. jails awaiting the outcome of threatened deportations—a 245 percent increase just in

the five years since adoption of the anti-immigrant legislation.

• Last year, once again with bipartisan backing, the Clinton administration cynically exploited its half-year-long refusal to return the Cuban child Elián González to his country in order to burnish the image of the INS and establish legal precedents reinforcing the agency's powers that are exempt from judicial review. The April 2000 raid by heavily armed commandos of *la migra* to take the child from a home in Miami not only bolstered the powers of the Border Patrol but dealt a blow to the Fourth Amendment rights of all U.S. residents to be safe from arbitrary searches and seizures.

• During his closing days in office Clinton issued a presidential directive establishing a "counterintelligence czar," and Bush just this week made an appointment to the new top-level spy post. According to press accounts, the position is "designed to facilitate a level of cooperation never seen before among the FBI, the CIA and the Pentagon, and will, for the first time, engage the rest of the government and the private sector as well." *The private sector as well?* What "private sector" police agencies are included? What strikebreaking rent-a-cops will now have more federal cover and encouragement?

The "czar" will be responsible to a board consisting of top CIA, FBI, Pentagon, and Justice Department officials and will in turn chair a National Counterintelligence Policy Board also involving officials of the State Department, Energy Department, and White House National Security Council. The former top CIA official who developed the so-called Counterintelligence for the 21st Century plan explained to one publication that "CI-21" will prioritize "the 'crown jewels' of American prosperity and national security," and told the *Washington Post* that it aims to defend "not only critical government assets but also the computer infrastructure used by government and private industry alike."

One reporter for the big-business press covering the new position wrote that it will force "the American public to rethink long-accepted notions about what constitutes national security and the once-clear boundaries between domestic law enforcement, foreign intelligence gathering and defense preparedness."

In short, the counterintelligence czar will draw together Washington's "anti-terrorist" operations from Iran, Korea, and Cuba, to the new immigrant living down the block. It will draw together the U.S. rulers' "war on drugs" from the new U.S. military bases in Colombia and Ecuador to working-class neighborhoods and factory locker rooms across North America. It will centralize the U.S. government's informers, wiretapping, snail-mail and e-mail snooping, and other secret police operations against both "enemies" abroad and the labor movement and social protest organizations at home.

Whether it is "endangering national security" or "giving away business secrets," the U.S. rulers will work to find a frame-up charge that sticks.

I raise the Clinton and Bush administration's new counterintelligence czar not because there is reason to anticipate some tidal wave of repression right around the corner. But the U.S. rulers are already shifting gears from the last decade. They know they will face more and bigger battles as international capitalist competition drives them to slash wages, extend the workday, intensify speedup, cut social security protections, and crush the unions. And they are preparing to defend their class interests.

So it's worth saying a few words before closing about what labor needs to fight for in this country to defend the class interests of workers and farmers around the world.

■

Given the capitalist class's unchallenged domination of politics, the mass media, and education, together with the America First nationalist perspectives of the union officialdom, it's very easy for workers and farmers to think and function entirely within the framework of the legislation, court rulings, and executive orders of the twin bourgeois parties, the Democrats and Republicans.

Right now, for example, you can't turn on the television or open a newspaper without being barraged with Bush's tax cut proposal and modified versions of it promoted by various Republican and Democratic members of Congress. Given all the red tape in which the income tax has become increasingly wound up over the past half century—the instruction booklet for the simplest federal income tax form, *the very simplest*, is 33 pages!—it's no wonder many workers and farmers are attracted to the idea of a "flat tax."

Working people know the tax brackets for the wealthy are officially set at higher percentages—but we also know the law is intentionally crafted to resemble a piece of Swiss cheese. High-priced accountants and lawyers happily offer their services to those with wealth and readily utilize all the hidey-holes and shelters purposely written into the fine print throughout thousands and thousands of pages of tax code. The result, just as millions of workers suspect, is that no one with capital pays taxes at anywhere close to the rates we read about in the big-business dailies or hear about on TV. Many pay nothing.

Farrell Dobbs taught us that one of the high crimes of the labor officialdom is their collusion with the employing class in tangling up workers in red tape instead of mobilizing union power to protect workers' interests. Wage rates, hours, and conditions should be straightforward and transparent, Farrell said. No contract worth a damn needs to be more than a page long, two at most. Then organize the ranks to enforce it.

It's a similar story with taxes. Whenever the capitalist politicians start talking about "income tax reform," workers know they always end up with the short end of the stick. So the bourgeois nostrum that everyone should file a simple post card and pay at the same rate, whether your income is ten thousand dollars or ten billion—with no deductions, no exemptions—gets a hearing among working people. The simplification and transparency alone make it seem appealing, even if working people pay at the same rate as those better off.

The illusion, of course, is that there is some way—be it a "flat tax" or some other "tax reform"—to make the owners of capital pay without taking state power out of their hands through a revolution and establishing a workers and farmers government. Short of that, the capitalists will always find ways to shift the tax burden onto our shoulders.

Communist workers are for a heavily progressive or graduated income tax, as we have been ever since that demand first appeared in the *Communist Manifesto* more than 150 years ago. But under capitalism the concept of a graduated income tax has become so corrupted that nobody except a small number of class-conscious workers recalls that the bold, revolutionary demand raised by the modern workers movement was never meant to apply to wages or the modest earnings of working farmers, fishermen, or other toilers. *To the contrary.* The graduated or progressive tax, as raised in the *Communist Manifesto,* is a levy not on wages but on *income* from profits, dividends, interest, or rents, including the elevated salaries of middle-class professionals, supervisors, and managers. Workers and working farmers were to pay no taxes; the "graduation" was to begin at the lower end of those who live differently from the proletariat as a result of capital's exploitation of the labor of the great majority.

The truth is that between the time the federal income tax was first introduced in 1913 and the beginning of World War II, 95 percent of the U.S. population paid no income taxes. Working people were exempt. But all that changed nearly overnight with legislation introduced at the opening of the war by the Democratic administration of Franklin Roosevelt and adopted by the bipartisan Congress. By 1943 income tax withholding—to finance "our" war—was showing up for the first time on our wage stubs, and the rulers never looked back from there.

Working people under capitalism always appear to be confronted with the dilemma of choosing between two (or sometimes more) bourgeois candidates, two or more bourgeois solutions. Lesser-evilism is what the rulers, backed up by the labor fakers and middle-class misleaders of civil rights and women's organizations, present as the be-all and end-all of politics.

That's why it's important that communist workers right now find ways to present some very basic, immediate demands to defend the conditions and solidarity of the working class and other toilers in face of rising joblessness, deepening indebtedness, and the ever-present danger of ruinous bursts of inflation or financial panic. These are what worker-bolsheviks can offer our class as a proletarian alternative to being whipsawed between choices presented by the Democrats and Republicans.

• Workers should demand a massive program of government-funded public works to ensure jobs for all at union scale. In addition to providing productive work to the jobless, such a program is needed to build housing, schools, hospitals and clinics, daycare centers, public transportation, libraries, gyms, pools, parks, and other social infrastructure the capitalists are allowing to crumble rather than fund out of their profits.

• Labor must demand a shorter workweek with no cut in pay, binding on all employers as federal law. This would spread the available work around and allow workers, not just the capitalists, to enjoy the benefits of any advances in the productivity of *our* labor.

• The working class must fight to increase the minimum wage. Even with the increase in 1996, the buying power of the minimum wage today is still lower than it was in 1960—and a full $2.25 below its high point in 1968. Given the competition for jobs under capitalism, wage levels are set from the bottom up, not from the top down.

Moreover, this minimum wage must be *universal*, one that no worker is denied, whether in a factory or in a prison. Everyone must be guaranteed full health, disability, and pension benefits. That—not demanding a halt to "prison work programs that unfairly compete with free labor," as the AFL-CIO bureaucracy raises today—is the only way to fight the bosses' abuse of prison labor. That is the only way to promote working-class unity and solidarity, not sabotage it.

• Labor must demand, once again as federal legislation, that all wages be covered by full and automatic cost-of-living protection. The capitalists' efforts to pull themselves out of a downturn in sales and profits can spark sudden and unexpected inflationary explosions that devastate the living standards and any small savings of working people. The same automatic adjustments must be guaranteed for all pension, health, workers comp, welfare, and unemployment benefits.

• Labor must reach out for allies among working farmers, as well. We must join with farmers to demand a halt to all foreclosures. Instead of being driven more deeply into debt slavery, small farmers must have access to government-funded cheap credit. They must receive price supports from Washington large enough to cover their full production costs and guarantee a decent and secure living for themselves and their families.

• The working class and labor movement in the United States must demand that Washington and other imperialist government and financial institutions immediately cancel the foreign debt that has been imposed on the semicolonial countries. Total Third World debt today is over $2 trillion, much higher than at the worst point of the debt crisis of the 1980s.

As international finance capital has squeezed more and more wealth from the toilers of Asia, Africa, and Latin America to bolster their sagging profit rates, one hundred countries—a quarter of the world's population—have experienced a decline in per capita income over the past fifteen years; in sub-Saharan Africa per capita consumption is 20 percent lower than it was in 1980! More than 45 percent of the population of the earth survives on less than $2 a day, and 20 percent on less than $1 a day.

• Workers and farmers in the United States should demand that Washington lift all tariffs and other obstacles to trade and travel erected by the U.S. rulers. This includes the elimination of all "anti-dumping," "fair labor," "environmental protection," and other trade weapons wielded with often devastating consequences by the U.S. government under the banner of "free trade." This must be labor's demand, not support for the protectionist policies of finance capital and ever more onerous trade restrictions aimed at semicolonial countries and imperialist rivals, as proposed today by U.S. union officials and the middle-class leaderships of various environmentalist and so-called anti-sweatshop organizations.

The elimination of all tariff and nontariff barriers erected by the U.S. government has nothing in common with the rulers' demagogy about guaranteeing a "level playing field for all"— exploiters and exploited alike. Instead, by demanding cancellation of the Third World debt and opposing all measures used by the propertied classes to magnify the unequal terms of trade intrinsic to the world capitalist market, working people in the United States can strengthen our unity with the toilers of these countries in the international battle against our common enemy, the imperialist ruling families who exploit us all to maintain their wealth and power. We can deepen the effort to transform our unions into revolutionary organizations of the working class that will inscribe these internationalist demands on our battle flag.

■

We opened the foreword to Pathfinder's new book on the Bay of Pigs with a statement from a 1997 interview with Enrique Carreras, a division general in Cuba's Revolutionary Armed Forces who as an air force pilot in 1961 sank two of the invaders' supply ships and downed two of their planes. Carreras says that the October "Missile" Crisis in 1962 was a continuation of U.S. imperialism's defeat at Playa Girón. "The defeat they suffered there led them to risk an atomic war," he says. "Girón was like a bone sticking in their throats, something they don't accept to this day."

Carreras is right. Despite the speed and decisiveness of Cuba's triumph at Playa Girón, Fidel Castro emphasized in his April 1961 report to the Cuban people on the victory that "this does not mean the danger is past. Quite the contrary," he said. "We believe that the danger now is great, above all, the danger of direct aggression by the United States."

As we've seen, the Kennedy administration was organizing invasion plans virtually as Fidel spoke, within days of Cuba's victory. And in October 1962 they saw their discovery of nuclear-armed missiles in Cuba as the opportunity to carry out those plans.

What stopped them from doing so?

Why, nearly forty years later, have the U.S. rulers never again attempted an invasion of Cuba?

Some of you have probably seen the movie, *Thirteen Days*. It is not accurate, of course. The movie is an apology for the Kennedy brothers and a glorification of American "democracy." It's about the imperialist rulers of this country and the executive branch of their government. It's another one of their propaganda binges about themselves, their real world, with the American people absent.

One of many things you won't see or hear in the movie, for example, is Robert F. Kennedy's "joke" at an early White House meeting where CIA officials displayed photos of the missiles and described their range. "Can they hit Oxford, Mississippi?" the attorney general wisecracked. He was fed up with being pressed by civil rights demonstrators to send U.S. marshals and troops to the South to enforce desegregation, as he had just been obliged to do a few weeks earlier when James Meredith, who was Black, had been denied entrance to the University of Mississippi in Oxford.

That was the Kennedy brothers' attitude toward the civil rights movement. It was a big pain in the neck—a just cause in the long run, perhaps, but a diversion from fighting communism in the here and now. Can the missiles hit Oxford, Mississippi?

Even before I went to see *Thirteen Days,* however, one of the criticisms in most of the reviews I'd read got me thinking from a slightly different angle about the questions we're discussing. The reviewers zero in on the fact that the movie concentrates to such a degree on the virtual family closeness of John and Robert Kennedy with Kenneth O'Donnell—"We band of brothers three."

The real O'Donnell, as opposed to the movie character, the critics say, was just the White House appointments secretary. He was just an old college buddy of Robert Kennedy and a Democratic Party political crony from Massachusetts—part of the "Irish Mafia." He was never present at the top-level White House meetings where the Pentagon, CIA, Defense Department, and National Security Council officials advised Kennedy on what to do about the missiles. (And O'Donnell's son put up a lot of the dough for the filming! On that one, the critics may be onto something!)

But the reviewers miss the point. Kennedy's decision over that thirteen days to back off from his initial determination to invade Cuba was a *political* decision. It was a decision the Democratic administration came to based on its judgment of the political consequences at home, among the population of the United States. O'Donnell may not have had much to do with the decision. But it *was* a political decision. And whatever the script's many distortions, the fictional O'Donnell—as in real life, the political organizer of the Kennedy image and of their permanent election campaign—serves to bring out that political reality.

There's a wonderful scene where John F. Kennedy is meeting in the Oval Office with the members of the Joint Chiefs of Staff. Among them is Curtis LeMay, chief of staff of the Air Force, who is the "Dr. Strangelove" character in the movie; a few years later, in 1968, LeMay ran for vice president as George Wallace's running mate in what was to be the last stand for open Jim Crow segregationists in national electoral politics.

Kennedy asks the generals and admirals for their estimates of whether the missiles could be taken out by U.S. air strikes alone. After a couple of noncommittal replies from other officers, LeMay, with great enthusiasm, speaks up: "Mr. President, I guarantee you we can take out 90 percent of those missiles!"

From the look on Kennedy's face, you know what's going through his mind: "What about the other 10 percent? How many U.S. cities can they hit before we can do anything?" From that point on, there's no doubt that if there's going to be any U.S. military action against Cuba it's going to include an invasion to get "the rest" of the missiles.

That part, at least, gets at some of the truth. The only plans Kennedy ever seriously considered for a direct assault on Cuba in October 1962 revolved around an invasion. It was the chance he had been waiting for ever since his humbling defeat at the Bay of Pigs. The movie shows the reporters badgering administration officials about the big troop movements and concentrations in the South—a military mobilization too big to miss.

What the movie doesn't show, however, is the White House meeting on October 26 when Defense Secretary Robert Mc-Namara tells Kennedy that the Joint Chiefs of Staff expect very heavy casualties from an invasion of Cuba. The Pentagon estimated that U.S. forces would suffer up to 18,500 casualties during the first ten days of battle alone—that's more than were killed and wounded during the first five years of combat in the Vietnam War! And the Cuban generals we interviewed for *Making History* were unanimous in asserting that the Pentagon estimate was far, far below what the actual U.S. casualties would have been if Washington had attempted an invasion.

Once Kennedy knew the Pentagon's estimates, then the invasion became a different kind of question. The political consequences of such staggering losses would have been enormous in the United States, and Kennedy backed down from his plans.

Of course, you see none of this in *Thirteen Days*. The movie follows the received wisdom of all major accounts both by upholders of U.S. imperialism and of the Stalinist regime in Moscow alike—that the peace-loving Kennedy brothers and Nikita Khrushchev, acting with good sense, moderation, and Christian humility saved the world.

In fact, with the exception of a couple of scenes of Cuban antiaircraft gunners firing at U.S. overflights, the Cuban Revolution doesn't exist at all in *Thirteen Days*. Cuban workers and peasants, armed and mobilized in their millions, are nowhere to be seen.

But the truth is the opposite. Through their revolutionary determination to defend their country and their socialist revolution, those toilers were—and remain today—the main actors in staying Washington's hand.

The Socialist Workers Party and Young Socialist Alliance were mobilized here in this country, too, during those historic days. One of the talks included in *Capitalism's World Disorder* tells a little of that history. The talk was given in November 1992, a month after the thirtieth anniversary of the October Crisis, which had been the topic of widely viewed documentaries on several U.S. television networks. A number of us had been struck in watching all of these documentaries by a peculiar inaccuracy. As noted in that talk, "Each of them portrayed what was happening in the United States [in October 1962] as universal mass hysteria. But if you lived through the missile crisis as a political person, as a revolutionist, you know that was not true."

As a relatively new member of the SWP and YSA in those days, I explained, "I know from my own experience that there were thousands of people in the United States who worked round the clock to stop Washington from invading Cuba. . . . We saw there was space to do this, and we used it." No hysteria, no stocks of bottled water and canned foods, just calm and confident work. In the process, those of us in the party and YSA "won some new, young fighters to the communist movement who were strengthened and given greater staying power by the test of fire."

■

It's appropriate that this public celebration of the fortieth anniversary of the victory at Playa Girón and the victory of Cuba's literacy campaign coincided here in Seattle with a two-day working meeting of the national leadership of the Young Socialists. The members of that revolutionary youth organization look to the program and traditions of the communist party in this country, the Socialist Workers Party, as their guide. And the worker-bolsheviks in our party keep reaching out as equals to these new generations with communist politics and with common activity—just as V.R. Dunne and others reached out to those of us who first came to revolutionary conclusions at the opening of the 1960s.

And it's also important that joining us here in organizing this celebration are members of our organized supporters movement. As volunteers for the Pathfinder Reprint Project, they shouldered decisive responsibilities over the past month in producing *Playa Girón/Bay of Pigs: Washington's First Military Defeat in the Americas*—translating material from Spanish to English and from English to Spanish; scanning items to be run in the book; preparing the graphics; and formatting and proofreading the pages. From locations in cities and towns across North America and around the world, some 200 supporters are now taking on the digital preparation of new Pathfinder titles, in addition to the work they've been doing for more than two years to help keep the communist movement's entire arsenal of some 350 titles in print. And they are joining SWP and YS members in the effort to get these titles onto the shelves of bookstores, other retail outlets, and public libraries, as well.

These revolutionary books and pamphlets—the lessons earned with struggle and blood by working people the world over during the past century and a half—give the communist movement tremendous political leverage. With the sea change in working-class politics, and the historic weakening of Stalinism worldwide, we can take communist ideas to people in struggle virtually anywhere in the world and gain a hearing.

This is what's changing. A vanguard layer of workers and farmers in this country is becoming more confident from their common fighting experience and thus more open to considering radical ideas, including the program and strategy of the modern communist movement. Whether they know it yet or not, their own experience in life and struggle is bringing them closer to that of the workers and peasants of revolutionary Cuba.

As growing numbers reject in practice what the bosses have so long sought to convince us of—that it's futile to struggle, we'll only be weakened and crushed—more and more members of a workforce in ongoing transformation will take a lead from the example set by Cuban workers and peasants forty years ago. As the back cover of the new book puts it, they taught us that with "political consciousness, class solidarity, unflinching courage, and a revolutionary leadership that displays an impeccable sense of timing, it is possible to stand up to enormous might and seemingly insurmountable odds—and *win*."

Those who have fought for, defended, and advanced the Cuban Revolution for more than four decades are ordinary working men and women. Likewise there was nothing special about the young people in this country who in April 1961 stood up to bourgeois public opinion and said with courage and confidence: "The Cuban people will win!"

What is special is never the human material, but the times we live in and our degree of preparation. If we've worked together beforehand to build a disciplined, centralized workers party— with a program and strategy that advances the historic line of march of our class worldwide—then we'll be ready for new opportunities in the class struggle when they explode in totally unanticipated ways. We'll be prepared to build a mass proletarian party that can take on the capitalist rulers in revolutionary struggle and defeat them.

That is the most important lesson that every one of us can draw. That is the reason to become part of the communist movement, to join the Young Socialists and Socialist Workers Party.

What we've been discussing and celebrating here this afternoon should make us think a little more deeply about the political significance of the U.S. speaking tours of Cuban youth that the Young Socialists and Socialist Workers Party have been involved in helping to organize over the past decade. It should help us weigh the importance of our work alongside Cuban revolutionists in reaching out to those anywhere in the world who want to build an international anti-imperialist youth movement—including our work this year to organize participation by young people from the United States in the Second Cuba-U.S. Youth Exchange in Havana this coming July, and then the Fifteenth World Youth Festival in Algeria the following month.

It should make us appreciate more fully the significance of workers and farmers from the United States visiting Cuba, learning firsthand about the revolution from fellow toilers, and then coming back to talk about the lessons with working people in this country.

It should make us better understand what we accomplish by working with others to ensure Pathfinder has a booth at the Havana book fair each year, and by collaborating with fellow revolutionists in Cuba on books such as *Che Guevara Talks to Young People* or the one we're celebrating here today, and then getting them into the hands of as many workers, farmers, and youth as possible in this country and wherever else we can.

■

In the May 1961 talk we quoted earlier, Che Guevara made a point it's useful to end on. When the toilers across Latin America first heard about the U.S.-organized invasion sometime during the day on April 17, he said, they responded with tremendous solidarity but also often with a heavy heart. "The protests were enormous," he said. "The popular masses went out into the streets. But many believed that a beautiful Latin American dream was being ended. That we were at the beginning of another sad stage, where imperialism would once again exert all its power, its conqueror's arrogance, all the power it can unleash against the peoples. . . ."

But a few days later, Che said, "when they saw the definitive victory of the people, everyone in Latin America saw clearly that a great defeat for imperialism had taken place." Moreover, he said, they had learned in practice that "solidarity is not just a matter of demonstrations of sympathy or of throwing stones in front of an embassy, but of much more serious things. The people now knew it was possible to make a revolution, and it was possible to take power against imperialism's servants."

Che is right. After that victory by the Cuban people—that bone still sticks in imperialism's throat to this day—no meeting, no demonstration, no joint work of any kind in defense of the Cuban Revolution has ever again taken place in sadness. They are organized with joy, and with confidence in the future.

And the greatest joy comes from the confidence that what Fidel Castro told the world in March 1961 not only remains true four decades later, but now has fewer historic obstacles in its way: before there's a successful counterrevolution in Cuba, there will be a victorious socialist revolution in the United States.

Yes, right here.

Index

Playa Girón / Bay of Pigs

Washington's First Military Defeat in the Americas

FIDEL CASTRO, JOSÉ RAMÓN FERNÁNDEZ

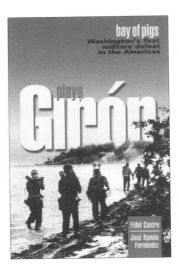

In less than 72 hours of combat in April 1961, Cuba's revolutionary armed forces defeated an invasion by 1,500 mercenaries organized by Washington. In the process, the Cuban people set an example for workers, farmers, and youth throughout the world that with political consciousness, class solidarity, unflinching courage, and revolutionary leadership, it is possible to stand up to enormous might and seemingly insurmountable odds—*and win*. Also in Spanish. $20

Pathfinder Was Born with the October Revolution

MARY-ALICE WATERS

Pathfinder Press traces an unbroken continuity to the pioneering forces who launched the world effort to defend and emulate the first socialist revolution—the October 1917 revolution in Russia. From the writings of Marx, Engels, Lenin, and Trotsky, to the words of Malcolm X, Fidel Castro, and Che Guevara, to those of James P. Cannon, Farrell Dobbs, and leaders of the communist movement in the U.S. today, Pathfinder books aim to "advance the understanding, confidence, and combativity of working people." Also in Spanish and French. $3.00.

The Working Class and the Transformation of Learning

The Fraud of Education Reform under Capitalism

JACK BARNES

"Until society is reorganized so that education is a human activity from the time we are very young until the time we die, there will be no education worthy of working, creating humanity." Also in Spanish, French, Swedish, Icelandic, and Farsi. $3.00

Making History

Interviews with Four Generals of Cuba's Revolutionary Armed Forces

Through the stories of four outstanding Cuban generals, each with close to half a century of revolutionary activity, we can see the class dynamics that have shaped our entire epoch. We can understand how the people of Cuba, as they struggle to build a new society, have for more than forty years held Washington at bay. Preface by Juan Almeida; introduction by Mary-Alice Waters. Also in Spanish. $15.95

Dynamics of the Cuban Revolution

A Marxist Appreciation
JOSEPH HANSEN

How did the Cuban Revolution come about? Why does it represent, as Hansen puts it, an "unbearable challenge" to U.S. imperialism? What political challenges has it confronted? Written as the revolution advanced from its earliest days. $22.95

Countermobilization: A Strategy to Fight Racist and Fascist Attacks

FARRELL DOBBS

In mobilizing labor, farmers, students, and others against assaults by racist and ultrarightist forces, says Dobbs, "the main thing is to educate a growing army of antifascists. The issue at stake for every fighter is: Are you going to be ready for the real thing when it comes? And it will come." $5.00

The Founding of the Socialist Workers Party

Minutes and Resolutions, 1938–39
JAMES P. CANNON AND OTHERS

At conventions and leadership meetings in 1938–39, revolutionists in the U.S. codified some two decades of experience in building a communist party. Taking the name Socialist Workers Party, they reaffirmed the Marxist approach in the fight against the coming imperialist war, the march of fascism across Europe, the battle against Jew-hatred, support for Puerto Rican independence, defense of the conditions of workers and exploited farmers, and the need for a proletarian party based in workers districts and the industrial unions. $20.95

The Struggle for a Proletarian Party
JAMES P. CANNON

A founder of the communist movement in the U.S. and leader of the Communist International in Lenin's time defends the proletarian program and party-building norms of Bolshevism on the eve of World War II. "The workers of America have power enough to topple over the structure of capitalism at home and to lift the whole world with them when they rise," wrote Cannon. $21.95

The Changing Face of U.S. Politics
Working-Class Politics and the Unions
JACK BARNES

Building the kind of party the working class needs to prepare for coming class battles—battles through which they will revolutionize themselves, their unions, and all of society. It is a handbook for workers, farmers, and youth repelled by the social inequalities, economic instability, racism, women's oppression, cop violence, and wars endemic to capitalism . . . and who are determined to overturn that exploitative system. $19.95

Lenin's Final Fight
Speeches and Writings, 1922–23
V.I. LENIN

In the early 1920s Lenin waged a political battle in the Communist Party leadership in the USSR to maintain the course that had enabled workers and peasants to overthrow the tsarist empire, carry out the first socialist revolution, and begin building a world communist movement. The issues posed in this fight—from the leadership's class composition, to the worker-peasant alliance and battle against national oppression—remain central to world politics today. $19.95 Also in Spanish.

The First Ten Years of American Communism
A Participant's Account
JAMES P. CANNON

"Stalinism has worked mightily to obliterate the honorable record of American communism in its pioneer days. Yet the Communist Party wrote such a chapter too, and the young militants of the new generation ought to know about it and claim it for their own. It belongs to them." — James P. Cannon, 1962. $19.95

Capitalism's World Disorder
Working-Class Politics at the Millennium
JACK BARNES

"Young fighters are attracted to the social weight and potential strength of the working class, its struggles, and its organizations. Growing numbers become interested in broader political ideas and join the communist movement." In four talks Jack Barnes explains the social devastation, financial panic, cop brutality, and drive toward fascism and war endemic to capitalism, and the power of workers and farmers, united in struggle, to reconstruct the world on new, socialist foundations. Also in Spanish and French. $23.95

Young Socialists Manifesto
"Our political program and activity stem from 150 years of the modern class struggle and the principles developed by the revolutionary workers movement," explains the Young Socialists in its statement of aims. In issue no. 11 of the Marxist magazine *New International.* $14.00 Also in Spanish, French, and Swedish.

Che Guevara Talks to Young People
"The individual effort, the purity of ideals, the desire to sacrifice for an entire lifetime to the noblest of ideals—all that is for naught if the effort is made alone," outside a revolutionary organization, explained Che Guevara to Cuban youth in 1960. One of eight talks from 1959–64 in which the legendary communist leader challenges youth to politicize their organizations, join in revolutionary struggles, and become a different kind of human being as they strive with workers and farmers of all lands to transform the world. Also in Spanish. $14.95

Teamster Rebellion
FARRELL DOBBS

The story of the 1934 strikes in Minneapolis that helped pave the way for the industrial union movement. Dobbs, a 27-year-old coal-yard worker at the time, tells how he became part of the union's class-struggle leadership and was won to the communist movement. "I had come a long way politically in a little over a year under the impact of my experiences in the social crisis" of the 1930s, Dobbs writes. $16.95

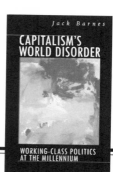

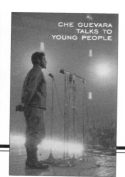

New International

U.S. Imperialism Has Lost the Cold War

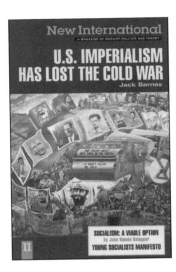

. . . That's what the Socialist Workers Party concluded at the opening of the 1990s, as regimes and parties across Eastern Europe and in the USSR that claimed to be communist collapsed. Contrary to imperialism's hopes, the working class in those countries has not been crushed. It remains an intractable obstacle to reimposing and stabilizing capitalist relations, one the exploiters will have to confront in class battles—in a hot war.

Issue no. 11 of *New International* analyzes the propertied rulers' failed expectations, assesses the weight of the Cuban Revolution in world politics, and explains why the odds in favor of the working class have increased, not diminished, at the opening of the 21st century. $14.00

Imperialism's March toward Fascism and War
JACK BARNES

"There will be new Hitlers, new Mussolinis. That is inevitable. What is not inevitable is that they will triumph. The working-class vanguard will organize our class to fight back against the devastating toll we are made to pay for the capitalist crisis. The future of humanity will be decided in the contest between these contending class forces."—Jack Barnes. In *New International* no. 10. $14.00

Opening Guns of World War III
Washington's Assault on Iraq
JACK BARNES

The U.S. government's murderous assault on
Iraq heralded increasingly sharp conflicts
among imperialist powers, the rise of rightist
and fascist forces, growing instability of
international capitalism, and more wars. In
New International no. 7. Also includes "1945:
When U.S. Troops Said, No!" by Mary-Alice
Waters. $12.00

Their Trotsky and Ours:
Communist Continuity Today
JACK BARNES

Following Lenin's death, the fight in the Bolshevik leadership to keep advancing along the
proletarian internationalist course he defended
was led by Leon Trotsky. By the late 1920s a
privileged social layer that came to be headed
by Joseph Stalin consolidated a political counterrevolution against Lenin's course within the
Soviet Union and Communist International.
Jack Barnes explains how Trotsky's ideas and
example help knit the continuity of communism,
from Marx and Engels's time to our own.
In *New International* no. 1. $8.00

The Rise and Fall of the
Nicaraguan Revolution

Lessons for revolutionists from the workers
and farmers government that came to power
in Nicaragua in July 1979. Based on ten years
of socialist journalism from inside Nicaragua,
this special issue of *New International* no. 9
recounts the achievements and worldwide
impact of the Nicaraguan revolution. It then
traces the political retreat of the Sandinista
National Liberation Front leadership that led
to the downfall of the revolution in the closing
years of the 1980s. Documents of the Socialist
Workers Party by Jack Barnes, Steve Clark, and
Larry Seigle. $14.00

MANY OF THE ARTICLES ABOVE CAN BE FOUND IN
NEW INTERNATIONAL'S SISTER PUBLICATIONS
IN SPANISH, FRENCH, AND SWEDISH.

Revolutionary leaders

The Communist Manifesto
KARL MARX AND FREDERICK ENGELS

At the end of 1847 two young revolutionists joined with veteran worker cadres from several countries to form the first modern communist organization. Its founding manifesto, drafted by Marx and Engels, declared that its program was derived not from "sectarian principles" but "from actual relations springing from an existing class struggle, from a historical movement going on under our very eyes." $3.95

To Speak the Truth
Why Washington's 'Cold War' against Cuba Doesn't End
FIDEL CASTRO AND CHE GUEVARA

In historic speeches before the United Nations and UN bodies, Guevara and Castro address the workers of the world, explaining why the U.S. government so hates the example set by the socialist revolution in Cuba and why Washington's effort to destroy it will fail. $16.95

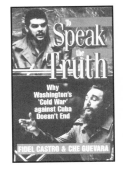

Malcolm X Talks to Young People

"I for one will join in with anyone, I don't care what color you are, as long as you want to change this miserable condition that exists on this earth" — Malcolm X, December 1964. Also includes his 1965 interview with the *Young Socialist* magazine. $10.95

Fertile Ground: Che Guevara and Bolivia
A FIRSTHAND ACCOUNT BY RODOLFO SALDAÑA

Told by one of the Bolivians who joined ranks with Guevara, Saldaña talks about the unresolved battles of the tin miners, peasants, and indigenous peoples of his country that created "fertile ground" for Guevara's revolutionary course and mark out the future of Bolivia and the Americas. $9.95

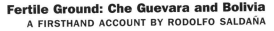

in their own words

The History of the Russian Revolution
LEON TROTSKY

The social, economic, and political dynamics of the first socialist revolution as told by one of its central leaders. "The history of a revolution is for us first of all a history of the forcible entrance of the masses into the realm of rulership over their own destiny," Trotsky writes. Unabridged edition, 3 vols. in one. $35.95

The History of American Trotskyism
Report of a Participant, 1928–38
JAMES P. CANNON

"Trotskyism is not a new movement, a new doctrine," Cannon says, "but the restoration, the revival of genuine Marxism as it was expounded and practiced in the Russian revolution and in the early days of the Communist International." In this series of twelve talks given in 1942, James P. Cannon recounts a decisive period in the efforts to build a proletarian party in the United States. $18.95

Rosa Luxemburg Speaks
EDITED BY MARY-ALICE WATERS

From her political awakening as a high school student in tsarist-occupied Poland until her murder in 1919 during the German revolution, Rosa Luxemburg acted and wrote as a proletarian revolutionist. *Rosa Luxemburg Speaks* takes us inside the political battles between revolution and class collaboration that still shape the modern workers movement. $26.95

Thomas Sankara Speaks
The Burkina Faso Revolution, 1983–87

Peasants and workers in the West African country of Burkina Faso established a popular revolutionary government and began to combat the hunger, illiteracy, and economic backwardness imposed by imperialist domination. Thomas Sankara, who led that struggle, explains the example set for all of Africa. $19.95

Cosmetics, Fashions, and the Exploitation of Women

JOSEPH HANSEN, EVELYN REED, AND MARY-ALICE WATERS

How big business plays on women's second-class status and social insecurities to market cosmetics and rake in profits. The introduction by Waters explains how the entry of millions of women into the workforce during and after World War II irreversibly changed U.S. society and laid the basis for a renewed rise of struggles for women's emancipation. $14.95

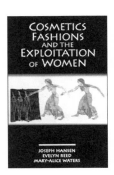

Fighting Racism in World War II

C.L.R. JAMES, GEORGE BREITMAN, EDGAR KEEMER, AND OTHERS

A week-by-week account of the struggle against lynch-mob terror and racist discrimination in U.S. war industries, the armed forces, and society as a whole from 1939 to 1945, taken from the pages of the socialist newsweekly, the *Militant*. These struggles helped lay the basis for the rise of the mass civil rights movement in the subsequent two decades. $20.95

The Origin of the Family, Private Property, and the State

FREDERICK ENGELS, INTRODUCTION BY EVELYN REED

How the emergence of class-divided society gave rise to repressive state bodies and family structures that protect the property of the ruling layers and enable them to pass along wealth and privilege. Engels discusses the consequences for working people of these class institutions — from their original forms to their modern versions. $17.95

Understanding History

Marxist Essays
GEORGE NOVACK

How did capitalism arise? Why and when did this exploitative system exhaust its once progressive role? Why is revolutionary change fundamental to human progress? $16.95

Maurice Bishop Speaks

The Grenada Revolution and Its Overthrow, 1979-83

Speeches and interviews by the central leader of the workers and farmers government in the Caribbean island of Grenada. With an introduction by Steve Clark. $24.95

Revolutionary Continuity

Marxist Leadership in the United States
FARRELL DOBBS

How successive generations of fighters took part in the struggles of the U.S. labor movement, seeking to build a leadership that could advance the class interests of workers and small farmers and link up with fellow toilers around the world.

VOL. 1: *The Early Years, 1848–1917* $16.95
VOL. 2: *Birth of the Communist Movement, 1918–1922* $16.95

Communist Continuity and the Fight for Women's Liberation

Documents of the Socialist Workers Party 1971–86

EDITED WITH AN INTRODUCTION BY MARY-ALICE WATERS

How did the oppression of women begin? What class benefits? What social forces have the power to end the second-class status of women? Why is defense of a woman's right to choose abortion a pressing issue for the labor movement? This three-part series helps politically equip the generation of women and men joining battles in defense of women's rights today. 3 volumes. $30.00

Out Now!

A Participant's Account of the Movement in the United States against the Vietnam War
FRED HALSTEAD

The political fight for a course that could organize in action the maximum number of working people, GIs, and youth and help lead the growing international opposition to the Vietnam War. Gaining momentum from the fight for Black rights, the antiwar movement helped force the U.S. government to bring the troops home, spurring struggles for social justice and changing the political face of the United States. $30.95

The Jewish Question

A Marxist Interpretation
ABRAM LEON

Traces the historical rationalizations of anti-Semitism to the fact that Jews — in the centuries preceding the domination of industrial capitalism — emerged as a "people-class" of merchants and moneylenders. Leon explains why the propertied rulers incite renewed Jew-hatred today. $17.95